The Four Oaks
A Biography of the Forshaw Family

The Four Oaks

A Biography of the Forshaw Family

The Lutterworth Press

Cambridge

The Lutterworth Press
PO Box 60
Cambridge
CB1 2NT

British Library Cataloguing in Publication Data:
A catalogue record for this book is available from the British Library

ISBN 0 7188 2917 4

Printed in Great Britain by
St Edmundsbury Press

Contents

List of Illustrations

Acknowledgements

The writing of this book could not have been contemplated, had I not the privilege of many visits over a long period to the late Richard Forshaw, whose self-effacing modesty, intellectual honesty and detached and seemingly surprised amusement at what was stored in his remarkable memory, together with a refusal to embroider any recollection, made him the ideal source of oral history as well as the provider of documents. Two of his sons, Bill and Fred, in the same mould, have been constant in their encouragement and advice and in tying up many loose ends. The book owes much to their generosity and that of their brother Edward and cousin David.

Even so, without the help of Mrs Mabel Roger, the youngest of Tom Forshaw's daughters, I would have remained largely helpless. Her reliable memory of the family and familiarity with the Carlton scene from the early 1920s has put me on the right lines on many matters.

The late Charlie Butler and Fred Miles, first-class horsemen and sound judges of their fellow men, have added much that perhaps only former employees could be expected to provide.

For information, including the loan of documents, on local matters I have been indebted to a host of people, but especially Margaret Warwick, Annie Overend, and Esme Greenwood (Burley) and Enid Oakes (Blyth). The staff of several public libraries have been unfailingly helpful, as has the Clerk to the Justices, Pudsey and Otley Petty Sessions and others in public office.

For the bare bones of the narrative, on which so many have helped to put the flesh, I have relied on the material I have collected since 1963 as honorary historian of the Shire Horse Society.

I record my thanks to the following for the supply of pictures: Mrs M M Roger (figures 1, 14, 16, 20, 22, 24, 26, 27, 28, 30, 42, 46, 48, 49); Bill Forshaw (21, 23, 25, 29, 36); Fred Forshaw (43, for copying pictures in possession of his brother and for supplying many others for deposit in the Shire Horse Archive); Pat Knowles (6); Enid Oakes (9, 11); David Curtis (31, 32); John Young (34, 50); and the City of Salford Cultural Services Department (12). Other pictures are reproduced by permission of Chorley Public Library (5), Ilkley Public Library (8) and the ILN Picture Library (17, 19). The remaining eighteen were already in my possession.

Preface

"If you want to know who we are," they sang as the curtain rose, "we are gentlemen of Japan". Only W S Gilbert could have been inspired to this way of beginning a piece which the audience already knew was called The Mikado. In a book entitled The Four Oaks, immediate explanation of who they were is not just a little joke but a necessity. Its sub-title shows that they were gentlemen called Forshaw, but this is simply a tautology, for that is what their name means.

In three generations, they were Shire stallion proprietors of such eminence that only Robert Bakewell himself stands above them. And their fame, unlike his, was to spread throughout the United States, Canada, Argentina, Australasia and elsewhere in the world. Furthermore, the scale of their operations, a matter of awe among their contemporaries, was beyond anything that Bakewell in the second half of the eighteenth century could have imagined to be possible. However, the horse age, when it ended, became so suddenly stone dead that, even though its final stage lies within the memory of many still living, the Forshaw name – like the excellence for which it stood – is now almost totally forgotten.

In recalling it, I do not have horsy readers in mind. Nor are these pages properly a biography, because too many of them are devoted to other people. Edward VII and George V come into it, as does Cuzzy Wood in his collarless grandad shirt and boots encrusted with dung. So do the Taylors, whose father died with a box full of sovereigns under his bed, and the 1st Lord Rothschild, who had a bank to keep his money in. Gwen Webb-Peploe, daughter of the Vicar of Christ Church, Cheltenham, forces her way in and John Roberts, who shot his cockerel to teach the bugger a lesson, is pushed into it by naughty boys. In the horse age, all sorts and conditions of men (and Miss Webb-Peploe) were intimately involved in the breeding of Shires. I therefore offer this book as a small and unsophisticated contribution to our social history.

The first eleven chapters follow a chronological sequence. The next four, introducing a few of those who worked for the Forshaws or had dealings with them, are topical in arrangement and are more or less confined to the twenty-one years between the end of the first war and the beginning of the next – the only period for which first-hand evidence and reminiscence is available. Chapter 16 is devoted to a small selection of equine characters. Almost nothing is said of their pedigree or of bloodlines, important though they were. Anyone with a mind to read that sort of thing must refer to my enormously long breed history, but for most of us the lives and eccentricities of people are more interesting than dead horses.

The last chapter is nearly all doom, death and destruction – or, if one views history from a different standpoint, it heralds the age of complete mechanisation in which Forshaws have turned their energies to other matters and life is so much easier for most of us, because we do not have to cope with the hardships of the natural world.

Fig.1 Tom Forshaw, the second and longest-living Oak, 1865-1955

1. Grandfather

It was just before noon on 18th June 1815 that Napoleon launched his ferocious attack on the British near the little Belgian village of Waterloo. At that very moment, we may be sure, in the yard of some village inn in the Fylde of Lancashire, George Forshaw's groom and his cart stallion were preparing for their midday bait – unless of course the taking of refreshment was delayed by a mare already awaiting attention. The horse would prefer to gratify his sexual appetite first.

As the two went on their way in the afternoon, the Duke of Wellington's men grimly held out against repeated cavalry assaults. The arrival of Blücher and the Prussians turned the tide and by nine in the evening the defeat of the French had become a rout. The horse was safely lodged at some other inn and, as the enemy were chased and repeatedly hammered throughout the night, his leader slept.

All we really know of George Forshaw is that he was born in 1771 at Aughton not far from Morecambe, that his wife Mary came from Up Holland nearly forty miles to the south and that he was now farming between these two places at Walton-le-Dale, east of Preston and between the Ribble and Darwen rivers. The name of his horse as of all his later ones is unrecorded, but the date is certain. It was to become an accepted fact, often repeated and therefore not subject to doubt, that grandfather first sent out a public stallion in the year of Waterloo.

If we call his horse a Shire, we can picture its shape, size and substance, but commit an anachronism. Seventy years were to pass before this label was adopted. The "Shire" of 1815 was the Black, which had originated, as a result of regular importations of Dutch and Flemish stallions, in the mists of the Fens, where it was huge, coarse, sluggish and soft. As it spread slowly westward, parish by parish, it became gradually harder-boned, less gross and more durable.

George Forshaw's enterprise owed everything to the work, in his own early years, of two great men. The name of Robert Bakewell of Dishley in Leicestershire is (or used to be) familiar to schoolchildren as a genius of stockbreeding, but he also succeeded, by precept and example in thirty years before his death in 1795, in transforming other men's understanding and practice in the matter of the Black horse and this was of more lasting importance. John Chadwick at Grindon, high and remote on the Staffordshire moors, was one of his disciples and in 1801 took the risk of sending his five year old stallion Packington, bred at Breedon-on-the-Hill, less than eight miles from Dishley itself, on a speculative three-month visit to the Warrington area forty miles away. This venture was a great success, though the horse afterwards blotted his copybook by slaying Joseph Thorns on 1st October.

Among the mares Packington had covered that season was one belonging to Joseph Battersby of Winwick. Next spring she produced an outstanding daughter which in 1808 he put to Chadwick's latest offering, Farmer's Glory.

Fig. 2 Robert Bakewell (1725-1795) was descended from Henry II's Chancellor. The fifth successive Robert in the family, he followed his grandfather and father as tenant of Dishley Grange, near Loughborough.

The result was a colt so good that he was left entire and became Battersby's Drayman, the first acknowledged Black stallion (more accurately, three-quarters Black) to be bred in Lancashire. The missionaries from Grindon were rapidly converting a county which, more than almost any other, had urgent need of powerful horses for industrial haulage. It is a reasonable guess that George Forshaw's first stallion sprang from the same source as Drayman.

Chadwick had done more for Lancashire than to send stallions there. He had introduced it to the modern method of breeding. The simple old way of shutting an oestrous mare in a little paddock with a horse, or of putting in half a dozen mares and removing each of them after she had been observed to accept him a few times, had now been superseded in the midlands and fens by a system based on a recognition not only of the stallion's remarkable ability to constantly renew his resources, but also of the obvious fact that variety was the spice of his life. Left with one mare on heat, he would mount her at increasingly long intervals, but a fresh one would immediately rekindle his desire, just as when a man has eaten his fill of beef, he will address himself with relish to a pudding. So, having learned from Bakewell, Chadwick was one of the new race of professional stallion-owners, whose horses were expected to cover up to a hundred mares, or even more, in the thirteen-week breeding season.

The idea was not new. Mithridates VI of Pontus had 30,000 brood mares which were served by a mere 300 stallions – or so the geographer and historian Strabo tells us, and he should have known. He was born there in 64 BC, the year before the king was finally defeated by the Romans and committed suicide. However, a practice which was simple in the vast military breeding establishments of ancient Pontus was more complicated when applied to modern England where the mares, scattered in twos and threes on the little farms, were primarily workers who produced foals, if they could, in their spare time.

Nowadays therefore the stallion, based either at home or, as in John Chadwick's case, at a far distant inn, set out on Monday mornings and walked a more or less circular route of anything up to seventy miles, returning to his headquarters at about midday on Saturdays. His stopping-places were advertised on posters nailed to trees and, increasingly, on cards handed out at markets or even printed in the local newspapers. This publicity also stated the fee for service and included a highly-coloured eulogy of the horse's talents and pedigree. The latter sounded impressive, even if most mare-owners knew no more of the animals listed in it than Chadwick or Forshaw knew of Mithridates.

Mares at farms actually on the route could be served by appointment at home, but all within the circle or not far outside it had only to be walked to the nearest point of the horse's passing. If necessary they could cut across the circle to intercept him on, say, a Tuesday instead of awaiting his arrival on the Friday, when it might be too late. Midday breaks were usually timed to last an hour, and the horse did not leave his overnight inn until 9am, in order to accommodate farmers who preferred him to have revived his spirits after a good rest. There was only one universal rule, unfailingly advertised: "No Business on Sundays".

To enable the groom to keep to his timetable, each mating had to be

Fig. 3 In John Chadwick's time and long afterwards, leaders of public stallions not uncommonly rode a pony.

consummated as speedily as possible. The gradual development of mutual desire by a stallion and mare living socially together was replaced by a sudden confrontation of strangers. This was fraught with danger. It was not in the nature of the mare to accept the horse at a moment's notice, even if she was in full heat. He, on the other hand, was ready almost instantaneously because he travelled alone and never met a mare except when invited to serve her. Therefore, a new method of in-hand mating had to be adopted, one man holding the mare and the other the horse.

Intelligent farmers benefited mightily from the new system. Their mares could be served, with only the slightest interruption of their daily work, by a top-class horse, almost certain to get foals that were better than their mothers. All the males could be sold off soon after weaning to other farmers whose practice was to grow them on, castrate them at two years, train and work them on their own farms and finally make a good profit when selling them at five years of age to meet the ever-increasing demand for good draught horses in the towns. Furthermore, the mare-owner knew exactly what he had to pay – a guinea or perhaps one and a half the first time, nothing at all for subsequent services at intervals of about three weeks if they were needed, and half a crown as a personal fee for the groom. This does not mean, of course, that there were no stupid or miserly men who preferred to use a handy scrub-stallion owned by an equally ignorant neighbour.

The stallion-owner's expenses were not insignificant – the leader's wages, board and lodging for horse and man, frequent shoeing. In addition the stallion ate the bread of idleness for nine months of the year. Before a profit could be shown, a proportion of the purchase price had to be recouped. This was usually estimated as at least one third in each season. Depreciation was one consideration, accelerated by the wear and tear on the horse in walking anything up to nine hundred miles in the season, the strain on his hind legs as he raised his great bulk to mount mares perhaps two hundred times and the shock transmitted to his front ones as he dismounted. More incalculable were the dangers that lurked at every turn, such as lameness, a venereal disease caught from an infected mare or a kick from a wild one. If for any of these or other reasons a horse was incapable of continuing his work, a substitute of equal quality had to be sent out as soon as possible if custom was not to be diverted to a rival.

On the other hand, a popular stallion that suffered no mishaps became a goldmine after his purchase price had been recovered. Success or disaster ultimately depended on the competence and character of the groom, especially if the route was not home-based. He was alone with a potentially lethal animal, solely responsible for his charge twenty-four hours a day, seven days a week for three months, without ally or adviser, since the rural horse-doctor at that time was unlikely to be any more knowledgeable than he was. In years to come the advance of veterinary science and the advent of the railways, telegraph and telephone were to be of enormous benefit to the Forshaws and other stallion-owners, but their reputation did not cease to be either made or marred as much by their seasonal employees as by the quality and fertility of their horses.

2. Father

George and Mary Forshaw's son Thomas was only two years old at the time of Waterloo. When he was twenty-four and Victoria had just become Queen, he married Margaret Wiggans of Leyland and took the tenancy of Billinge Farm, Eccleston. Lancashire boasted three Ecclestons and this one was four miles from Chorley. From the windows of their rambling old house or the quiet garden, the couple could look out at their good rich land running down to the Yarrow river. On the opposite bank stood the ancient church and village.

Eccleston was then, before any mill was built, still much as it had been for a hundred years or more. There was no squire and most of the landlords of the district were Catholics. Consequently, many of the ordinary folk were Catholics too. Nevertheless, the 770 or so inhabitants lived together without noticeable disharmony, in what a later rector was pleased to describe as godly obscurity. Like the several other Forshaw families in those parts, including three which farmed in the neighbouring parish of Croston, Thomas and Margaret had no truck with popery, and so the Rev William Yates duly baptised their first child Mary, after her paternal grandmother.

Before his marriage Thomas appears to have acted as stallion-leader for his father, who was now nearly seventy. Practical expertise of what that difficult job entailed was no doubt of incalculable benefit to him as he took over the business and increased its scope. He was soon the proprietor of three or four entire horses, and certainly knew exactly what to look for in those he employed to travel them. Since the outstanding success of the next three generations of Forshaws depended on such men almost as heavily as on the horses they led, it is perhaps appropriate here to summarise the virtues to be sought in a travelling groom. There were six, of which four were essential.

The first quality, obviously, was horsemanship and this necessarily included dedication to the work. The stallion's needs had priority – day in, day out, every early morning, every late evening. Sweating in the heat, wet after downpours of rain, tired, hungry or out of sorts the man might be when they arrived at their lodging for the night, but so was the horse. He had to be attended to first, methodically and thoroughly. The groom was his only companion and had to be his friend. He also had to be his lord, since a stallion inherits the age-old instinct that he ought to be master of all he surveys – as indeed in the wild he once was, provided that he could dominate potential rivals. In domestication he had to learn that this was not the case. A human being, whom he could easily demolish within seconds, was the boss. The groom had therefore to exercise unremitting discipline and to be always predictable in his reactions to misdemeanour. The good schoolmaster can relax with his pupils if he likes or even lark about – and, when he wishes, instantly return to the master-pupil relationship. Even a boy could understand the situation – but a horse could

Fig. 4 The farm house at Eccleston was built in 1750 by Robert Billinge. The upper windows may have been already bricked up in Thomas Forshaw's time, as here. In more modern times the top storey was removed and the building extended laterally.

not. If he had done something he ought not to have done and had got away with it, he would interpret tolerance as weakness. However, if the groom attempted to maintain his position by any act that involved cruelty, he would fail in the end. The horse would not forgive him, but patiently wait for that moment of carelessness that enabled him to get his own back, with interest. He could interpret a smack on the nose as a punishment if it was administered instantaneously, but he could not associate it with something he did wrong a few minutes before. He would merely wonder what the silly man had hit him for. The horse could be out of sorts and behave accordingly. The groom had to be as immutable as God – who, in the horse's mind, he was.

The travelling man had also to know more about mares and their ways than their owners themselves usually did. His decision as to whether one was ready or fit to be served was final. It was he, not his customer, who was in command at the covering. At every stage, he had to work on the principle that a mare-owner might prove to be a fool, and quite often he did.

The second requirement was fitness and resilience. Ideally, he was a short chap because that made his horse look all the more huge and beefy, but if he was, that was simply a bonus, He had to walk as far as the horse did. At matings, his work was sometimes onerous, even if not so strength-sapping as that of his companion. He had to do all the thinking for two or four. If he met aggressive characters on his way, he had to be able to deal with them, though his companion was a redoubtable ally whom only an idiot would challenge. However, if these were gypsies who fancied a free service for one of their mares, he had to be wise enough to accede without demur, for he had no hope of winning. The stallion, unaware that a fee should be charged for his pleasure, would change his allegiance unhesitatingly. In Thomas Forshaw's time, service fees were always paid in cash – but their protection was the least of the leader's worries. If placed in a bag attached to his horse's bellyband, money was safer than in a bank. At night, it could be put in a far corner of the loose box. There was no better guard against robbers than a ton of stallion.

The safeguarding of cash leads naturally to its collection in the first place and to the third necessary attribute of the travelling man, honesty. There was simply no means by which an owner could assure himself that the money brought home represented the number of services performed. Other kinds of salesmen could be held to account by checking the takings against the goods unsold – but the groom was only selling semen and the stallion made that as he went along. The most straightforward fraud was the half-price service, never declared at all. If the correct fee was two guineas plus two shillings groom's fee, the mare owner would then pay one guinea and save £1-3-0 and the man would pocket the guinea and waive the personal fee, making a profit of nineteen shillings. Or a customer might offer two mares on condition that a third was served free. Rather than forfeit all business with such a fellow, the groom would be tempted to take his three florins and defraud his master of two guineas. But what about six for the price of four – a big deal, terms negotiable? Did they really all belong to the one customer? Or was he acting as a middleman for neighbours?

Prudent stallion-owners had learned to provide a little book in which each service and the fee paid were recorded and the entry signed by the farmer who was thus prevented from claiming that his mare had never been served at all or that, although she had not held to it, the groom had failed to bring the horse again. But it was not infallible. If the farmer could not write, a cross was poor evidence. And the book was not proof against his producing a second mare for a free service three weeks later, alleging that it was the same one as before – though this could never fool a competent groom who could remember the individuality of all the mares covered by his horse that season. If, on the other hand, the farmer was honest but doubted the leader, he would ask for the book to prove that he had paid up. But where there was collusion, the book was useless.

However, we must not overstate the possibilities of fraud. In the season, a travelling man was paid more than any other farm employee. In addition, a hundred personal fees amounted, at two shillings a time, to an extra £10 or to £12-10-0 at half-a-crown – fantastic wealth in itself. On top of all, there was often a bonus if the horse was brought home in good condition. Some owners even offered a share of the service fee for every mare served above a hundred, but this incentive had to be balanced against the 'home in good condition' reward. The owner and the groom depended on each other and there was generally good faith, even a feeling of partnership, on both sides. In the last resort, if the owner suspected his groom's integrity, he would find another next season. A man was a fool if he risked the loss of such a profitable seasonal occupation. Since there were so many who served the same master for many seasons, one is led to believe that nearly all were honest to a degree that might seem surprising today.

The fourth characteristic of a good travelling man was salesmanship, especially if he was up against competition. In singing his horse's praises he had to be not only articulate but a quick and cunning judge of personality. His spiel to a brutish sort of person would be distasteful to Baptists, for whose favour he would present his horse as a Christian. He had to be all things to all men. Most leaders had a great gift of the gab, and it was useful to be a wondrous liar if he had a bad horse; but it was no use being a liar if the man you were talking to already knew you were.

With the fifth virtue, sobriety, we arrive at what was desirable rather than absolutely necessary. A sober man gives offence to none, but what was there to do in the evenings after the horse had been bedded down? And how could a man drink nothing at his advertised daytime ports of call? And were not the farmers hospitable when he called? After a successful mating, was it not churlish to refuse a celebration? Towards the end of the day's march, inebriation might set in, but if a man got to the point of inability to walk unaided, he had simply to slip his hand under the stallion's bellyband and be carried scuffling along. A horse soon learned his route. Even if his master collapsed and lay incapable by the roadside, there would be no problem. A stallion has an innate sympathy for a friend in this particular form of distress. He would not rush off to create mayhem wherever he could find the opportunity to do so, but would stand protectively over him until he could rise again. And woe betide anyone who, whether with good or ill intent, attempted to approach!

The last of the virtues, and the least important, because a lack of it did not inevitably impair a man's performance of his proper work, was chastity. It was also the most difficult for him to preserve and, when he failed, he was far from wholly to blame. The cause of the trouble was his horse's sexual apparatus.

Other farm animals are equipped with a penis of the common fibroelastic type. That of the familiar bull, for example, is puny and runs along the underside of the belly, enclosed and hidden by his outer skin. Held back normally into an S-shape within that protection, the end of it scarcely protrudes from its orifice, about half way between his hind and his fore legs, until he mounts the cow, when it snaps out straight. The free part is thus short and thin and not much more rigid than it was before. Its weight is negligible and causes its owner no inconvenience. Copulation is easy, brief and not very energetic, since it is the warmth of the cow which causes just a single ejaculation.

The stallion, on the other hand, shares with the elephant, the rhinoceros, the curious tapir and a few others the privilege or handicap of possessing a penis of the vascular-muscular type. This kind is normally stored entirely within the body and, in the horse, is protected by a V-shaped sheath between its legs. An additional flow of blood is required to cause it to emerge into and then from this sheath and steadily enlarge it until it reaches a monumental length and diameter. Its great weight, totally unsupported except at its root, requires very powerful muscles to raise it, and this position can be sustained only briefly except under the most intense sexual excitement. When the mare is mounted, it depends on friction to bring about a series of five or six ejaculations. A further difference is that this type of penis can be drawn out and even erected at will, and in young animals often is. It does not require the presence of a mare or of any other apparent stimulus.

If witnessed by a member of the female sex, the business which the groom superintended, although perhaps filling some with disgust or even terror, notoriously and provably had a most powerfully stimulating effect on most. The spectacle of the horse as he prepared for his duty was an aphrodisiac which roused them to uncontrolled excitement. As the mare, raising her tail, presented herself to him, they identified with her. By the time all was over, they were swooning. It was universally recognised, and fully understood by grooms, that this experience would be likely to cause them to offer themselves to the first man they met afterwards.

On farms, anxious mothers would lock their daughters and maidservants in until the horse had left. When he was due to pass the wayside cottage, they would keep their girls within doors for a while, for a mare might be waiting at the crossroads and the ensuing hubbub would attract their attention. Working girls, as in the mill towns, were not under such restraint. They would learn to look out for the stallion as he approached his appointed stopping-place and accost the groom, expressing admiration for his charge. Could they stroke him? Was he safe? Where was he going and what was he going there for? If the answer was not clear they were free to find out. No other animal than the stallion could have such an extraordinary influence on common morals. If asked why, the girls would of course point to his sexual organ and his interesting ability to produce it at any time and wave it about. But there was more to it than that. The rhino or elephant, had they roamed the countryside on a similar mission, would have caused mere astonishment. But these are animals whose extraordinary shape and leathery hides are not physically attractive. In Scotland, a law was enacted to prohibit the serving of a mare in any public place or indeed any place where females and young boys might observe it. The inclusion of boys in the ban was absurd, for it was unenforceable. There never was a way of barring them from that sort of free show. If chased from a yard, they would reappear at the top of a wall. Removed from a gateway, they would climb a tree.

The stallion-leader acquired a sort of glamour. Stay-at-home men looked upon him with awe and envy as they might regard a fire-eater in the circus or a lion-tamer. All through the nineteenth century and half way into the twentieth, he was a favourite subject of anecdotes. One newspaper cartoon showed him coming across a country parson, who asked him if he was having a good season. The reply was tipsily jocular. "Not 'arf sir. We only been on the road two weeks, and I'm three ahead of 'e a'ready."

It would be obviously wrong to suggest that travelling grooms were all alike in their attitude to life. Joe Sobersides was a married man with several children. He arranged for his wages to be paid to his wife while he was away and he would come home with a nest egg to provide the family with a few comforts – new boots, perhaps, for the children and some pretty article of dress or a bonnet for their mother. He hoped to take a horse every year as long as his health and strength permitted. When his young had flown the nest, it would enable him to put by a little against old age. In the same mould was young Ernest, saving up to marry and rent a little holding of his own. Neither wasted their precious fees on drink or wavered in their strict morality. Jack Frothblower, on the other hand, was motivated by the opportunity to get away for three months from a sour and tyrannical wife to a land of liberty and liquour. Young Charlie-boy was happy-go-luckily experiencing the first flush of freedom from a bullying father and a strict mother. One day he might settle down and be like Joe or Ernest. You could never tell with young chaps. Meanwhile, a very presentable young man, he was the greatest threat of all to the young women in the parishes where he led his horse.

Margaret Forshaw had her second baby, a boy, on 16th November 1840, and he was duly christened James. Her husband very well understood the attributes of a good stallion-leader, but soon proved that he had no idea of what was required in a father. That is why James, when he grew up, never spoke about him. All he ever did in this respect was in his old age to dictate to one of his daughters a few scraps of information, sufficient only to give his family some knowledge of the start of his own career.

These notes give the impression that his parents remained at Eccleston until he was seventeen. This was not so. By 1847, William Marsden and his family occupied Billinge and the Forshaws have had to be tracked down to Dutch Barn Farm three and a half miles away, on the northern edge of Chorley – a little distance along the lane that turns off the Preston road and leads to Euxton. The 1851 Census shows Thomas (38) as a farmer of 66½ acres, employing three men; his wife Margaret (36); Mary (12), James (10) and Elizabeth Ellen (8), all born at Eccleston; and George (4) and little John Thomas (2) born at Chorley. Because Mary was old enough to help in the house, Margaret had only one domestic servant – Alice Latham (18) who was her, or perhaps her husband's, niece. There was also William Rigby (33), a farm servant living in. The household was completed by Thomas' aged parents. Unlike Billinge, the new house was heavy, foursquare and totally without charm. The awesome barn which gave the holding its name was of almost cathedralian height and its enormously heavy flagstone roof was supported by eight massive brick pillars linked by brick arches, on which lay great rough-hewn timbers running along and across. The farm belonged to the Townley-Parkers of Cuerdon Hall and Astley Hall.

Chorley was a fast-growing town. It had trebled in size during the first half of the century and its population was now about 14,000. There were twenty firms manufacturing muslin and cotton goods, one of them being Edward Tootal & Co. There were six cotton spinners and three calico printers. Bleaching works and coal mines abounded in the neighbourhood. Its communications were good. The Leeds and Liverpool Canal skirted the town, which was now connected by rail to Bolton, Manchester, Liverpool, Warrington and Lancaster. Less than a century before, it had been a little place with a single short, narrow twisting street. Now it supported three churches and the inhabitants were in turn supported by 35 inns, hotels and taverns, 34 beerhouses, five brewers and three coopers. There were 31 boot and shoe makers and 16 makers of clogs and pattens. Fairs were held six times a year, including the great three-day one in September, and there were two market days a week.

James was now attending the National School in Bolton Street under Mr Thomas Brown. His father believed in education as long as it did not interfere with work. James had worked, in every available moment, ever since he was capable of doing anything useful at all. He had never played. By the time he was eight, he was called every morning at four o'clock in summer and five in winter, and worked until school-time. On return from lessons, "I had to work again with the men, until my mother insisted on my going to bed. My father was a hard man. I can truthfully say that he discouraged every kind of recreation, and thought work was the only thing to be done when I was not actually at school or asleep." By the time he won a place at the Grammar School when he was eleven he knew as much about the practice of horse breeding as many men learned in a lifetime. He used every trick he could to ensure that his work was always in the stables and never among the cattle. When journalists in later years asked him, as they always did, how long he had been in the stallion business, he invariably trotted out one of his two stock replies – "From the hour that I was born," or "I was cradled among them." He never said more than that. He told no one except his daughter that in spite of the protests of Philip Briggs, the headmaster, he was taken away from the grammar school when he was twelve.

Fig. 5 Chorley Market Place. The Fazakerley Arms is in the centre behind the horse and cart in this 1872 picture.

During the covering season, while his former friends were at their books, he was now occupied with more pressing matters. For example, one of the Forshaw stallions was available on Tuesday market days at Chorley to serve mares from the surrounding countryside in the yard of the Fazakerley Arms, and it was James who now led him out of the stable for prospective customers to examine, and who acted as assistant at the mating. He therefore accustomed himself at a tender age to the interest which his work inspired among idle onlookers. The stallion on duty there in 1853 was Lancashire Hero, a five-year-old bred by Edward Haydock at Hesketh in the marshes south of the Ribble estuary only eight miles from Chorley. Its pedigree, so far as it can be reconstructed, goes back in one line to Dickenson's G. Dickenson was also a Lancastrian, at Culcheth, and G's single-letter name indicates descent, real or pretended, from Bakewell's most celebrated stallion. In other lines, Lancashire Hero can be traced to several of John Chadwick's horses including Packington himself.

The best of Thomas' horses that season was a grey one, Kirby, whose colour is a reminder that the infiltration of Blacks into newer districts in the past fifty years had caused many of them to have not only grey coats, but even bay and other colours. Kirby had been bred in Derbyshire and Thomas had acquired him as a three-year-old in 1851. His sire was a celebrated horse called Invincible, which to the confusion not only of contemporary mare owners in two or three midland counties but also of the historian today, was renamed Derbyshire Hero by his second owner the well-known Mr Stych of Stenson and Shropshire Friend by a third. His grandfathers also were noted stallions – Mr Stych's graphically but somewhat crudely named Bang-Up and an earlier Kirby, owned by J Lycett of Leek. This old Kirby began serving mares in 1831 and was still doing so, though at longer intervals, when he died of exhaustion twenty-five years later – a remarkable record. The Forshaw Kirby won seventeen prizes at shows in Lancashire and Thomas had his portrait painted in 1855. In 1857, when he was nine, someone came with a lot of money and bought him. So he left Dutch Barn Farm and went to Russia.

The same year, the Forshaws also left. Thomas, now 43, took the 128-acre Latus Hall farm in the parish of Goosnargh, twelve miles away on the other side of Preston. A long lane led to the house from the hamlet of Inglewhite, where until about 1800 both cotton and silk manufactures had thrived. But now, defeated by competition from steam power, the industry had dwindled to nothing, for Inglewhite had no coal near at hand and its water supply was inadequate. As Chorley grew and prospered, the whole parish of Goosnargh declined. The Hall took its name from one William Latus, a Catholic whose estate became forfeit to the King in 1607. One of two inscribed stones bears the legend ERAR 1654, a memorial that Edward Rigby and his wife then owned it. In 1726, James Parkinson had bought the place and rebuilt it as the pleasant five-bedroomed dwelling to which Thomas now brought his family and four new stallions.

Brown Stout, bred in Shropshire, was five and that summer had won first prize at the Manchester and Liverpool Show. Duke of Wellington, a four-year-

Fig. 6 Latus Hall has been little altered since the Forshaws' time or even since its rebuilding in 1726 by James Parkinson

old black, was Lancashire-bred shortly after the death of the hero of Waterloo. His dam had been sired by Thomas' own Lancashire Hero. Lord Raglan, also four years old and black, acquired his name a little late in honour of the British Commander-in-Chief in the Crimea. He was bred by a Mr Price of Willoughby in Leicestershire and his dam must have been an outstanding animal, for she was sold shortly afterwards for a very large sum which increased year by year in Price's memory until it grew beyond the belief of even his most credulous acquaintance. The name of the fourth newcomer harked back to an earlier national hero. Lord Nelson, bred near Warrington by John Taylor of Warburton, was seven and iron-grey. His pedigree – "Sire: Taylor's Old Lord Nelson; dam by Young Sheppard" – means nothing now and probably very little, except to J Taylor and T Forshaw, at the time.

In 1858, the year following the move, the Royal Show came to Chester. Thomas, keen to test his horses against the best in England, exhibited Duke of Wellington and Lord Raglan as "Agricultural Stallions" and Lord Nelson in the class for "Dray Stallions". (This distinction was as confusing as it was absurd, and owners were frequently in a dilemma as to which sort of horse they had.) None of the three won anything, but for the seventeen-year-old James, who did all the work of preparing them and also showed them in the ring, it was an educational experience.

That year his father also acquired a couple of two-year-olds. One of these, Champion King, was of orthodox Leicestershire breeding but Short Legs is of interest because he had been bred by Henry Draper a mile away across the Yarrow from Billinge Farm and was by Lord Raglan, which was himself only two at the time of conception. Ambitious stallion-owners (and Thomas, relying more and more on James's abilities, was certainly among them) were always ready to buy up promising colts or fillies got by their own horses and would pay a slightly inflated price for them in order to boost their reputation ("Have you heard how much so-and-so got for that foal by Forshaw's horse?" One man would ask another, and add "I think I'll use him myself next year"). In terms of hard cash, the profit from this ploy largely depended on an ability to look at a foal and see what he or she would be when adult. This is a rare gift and there is no reason to suppose that James, who possessed it in abundance when adult himself, did not reveal it at this stage in his life.

As he approached his nineteenth birthday, he took stock of his position. "I began to realise how hard my life was, and how difficult a man my father. I was to work all day and every day. On Sundays, as the men did not come, I worked harder than ever, and had a scramble to get done and dress in time for evening service at church. I came to the conclusion that I was worthy of a wage. Finally, I decided to mention the subject to my father who, so far, had never paid me anything, though of course I lived at home and he bought all my clothes. He very much resented the idea, and for a short time his overbearing manner mastered him." James was always good at understatement. What he meant was that Thomas flew into an uncontrollable rage. "I went to my mother and asked her to pack my things, as I was going away. She did so with many regrets, for she knew my decision was final and that I should not return to live at home again – or, at least, fate would have to be very unkind to me before I did."

His wretched fragments of reminiscence describe Margaret Forshaw as "a model housewife who kept everything spotless, being very methodical. Tall, with a very good figure and good to look at, she was quite a person to be noticed in any company wherever she happened to be, and I was indeed justly proud of her." Loyalty to mother, however, could not compete with the desire to get away from father. So he kissed her goodbye and pocketed his savings, which amounted to nine pounds and some coppers jealously hoarded from a few tips received while travelling stallions. Thomas had never quoted a groom's fee on his stud cards and advertisements, believing that the two shillings that his customers saved in that way were a further inducement to continue to use his horses, but just a few generous folk had from time to time pressed a coin into the son's palm in recognition of some special assistance beyond the strict call of duty.

In later afternoon, James walked to Preston station and asked for a ticket to travel on the next train.

"The next train to where?"

"Anywhere."

The man gave him a funny look. But this youth, six feet tall and powerfully built, was clearly determined. There was no point in raising any queries. So he sold him a ticket to Manchester.

3. Young Man in Wharfedale

In Manchester, James found a lodging for the night and, since he did not know the name of any other large horse-owning business, enquired his way next morning to Carver and Company, which he had heard men talking about at home. He found they were carriers and warehousemen, carting agents to the Lancashire and Yorkshire Railway Company, with depots in Liverpool and Bradford as well as Manchester. The manager interviewed him, took him to the stables, summed him up and told him to start work in the afternoon. He was sorry that there were no stallions to be found there, nor mares to be served. After this little joke, he said he could have the same wages as the older stablemen.

After six weeks and with equal suddenness, James was promoted to the position of head horseman. Not surprisingly, this was received by the others at first with resentment and jealousy. After all, some of the men now under him were three times his age and had been working there four hundred times as long. But his effervescent and somewhat crude sense of humour, his readiness to help anyone less intelligent and able than himself and his total lack of self-importance – qualities which marked him out in later life – must all have come to the surface as a result of his having at last found his own individuality. To quote again from his stilted fragments of reminiscence, "we went on very comfortably and smoothly for about two years".

During this time, he occasionally returned to Goosnargh to see his mother and brothers and sisters and to visit the one friend he had been able to make during his years of servitude. This was William Dagger, the youngest son of the family which farmed nearest to Latus Hall. William's sister, Mary Ann, was extremely good-looking and, although just over seven years older than James, still a spinster. This status was altered as a result of what happened one midsummer's evening. Emergency weddings were the norm in those parts, for when folk were taken by surprise at the calling of banns they explained their amazement by saying they "hadn't heard as 'er was big". They were married at Goosnargh and Mary returned there to have her baby, who was born on 7th March 1861. Not long after, "the Head told me he was going to move me to their branch establishment at Bradford, to get the stables into the same condition as those at Manchester and improve the class of horse by buying better ones. He was passionately fond of his horses and said that he must have them turned out second to none." So the baby, Margaret, was unofficially adopted by Grandmother Dagger and will play no active part in the Forshaw story. James "found both horses and stables at Bradford in a much worse condition than I expected, but I worked hard and, as time went on, they improved and were quite equal to the ones I had left."

When he had worked for Carver's four years altogether and accumulated a little nest egg, he broached the idea of setting up for himself and owning a

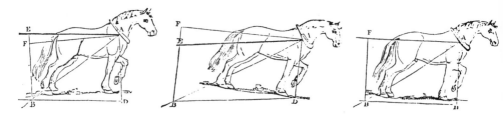

Fig. 7 (Above and opposite). At Carver's, James was familiar with Isambard Kingdom Brunel's treatise *On Draught*, first published in 1831 and frequently reprinted. The author's many sketches included these, which illustrate the correct angle of draught.

stallion. Mary Ann was horrified. That was not really a respectable means of livelihood. Her reaction was something of a surprise to James, especially as she knew that he had been employed in that way by his father. He failed to appreciate, as she did, that times were rapidly changing. The late-lamented Prince Consort had stamped his puritan ideas upon English society and there were all sorts of customs and activities which had become not quite the thing. The serving of mares in public places and the immoralities and licentiousness which this activity so often engendered among people of the looser sort still continued, but town life was something different. Their respectable acquaintances would not approve. What had been acceptable to Granny Forshaw in the year of Waterloo, or to Mrs Thomas Forshaw when she married in 1837, was really beyond the pale in the Bradford of 1863. In the end, Mary Ann withdrew her opposition, and he started to look for a place in the country that they could afford to rent. Their plans were slightly complicated by the fact that, after two years of marriage, Mary Ann was again big. In June 1863 she gave birth to her second child, baptised James Dagger, and her husband found just the sort of place he wanted at Burley-in-Wharfedale, eight or nine miles from the middle of Bradford.

"Burley," a commentator had written some twenty-five years earlier, "is a delightful village, though contaminated physically and morally by a cotton mill." Mr Speight, however, writing somewhat later, had been more enthusiastic. Messrs Greenwood and Whitaker's mill "performed a charitable work, being almost entirely run, overseers excepted, by children sent from workhouses in London who were apprenticed to the trade. When they had served their time many settled in the place and their families afterwards became comfortably off." This influx had enabled Burley at last to claim independence from Otley and in 1843 it had become a separate parish with a population of a little over 1700.

When Mr Jonas Whitaker retired from business in 1849 (before dying the following year), the property was bought by Messrs William Fison, his son-in-law, and W E Forster. These two, on borrowed capital, had set up a woollen business in Bradford seven years earlier and started their regime in Burley by organising a holiday outing for the workpeople in September. This event was believed, at least in the locality, to be the first ever laid on by factory bosses. Then they demolished the mill and built a new factory for worsteds. This contained a splendid dining-room for the workers. Their aim was to make the

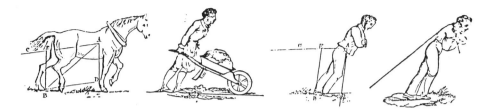

place a model of good order, cleanliness, contentment, godliness and profit. In view of all this, it is perhaps not surprising that Burley also claimed to be the first place in the dale to have a flower show, the first to hold an athletics meeting, the first to possess a lecture hall and the first to organise a Volunteer Corps, of which W E Forster was Captain.

William Edward Forster was always considered a "typical Yorkshireman", whatever that might mean. In fact he was born at Bradpole in Dorset, the only son of remarkable parents. His father William was a great Quaker philanthropist whose death in America in 1854, when reported in the press, had caused consternation both there and at home. Anne, his stunningly beautiful mother, was the sister of Sir Fowell Buxton MP, a partner in Truman, Hanbury, Buxton and Company, brewers of Spitalfields, a great benefactor of the poor in that parish, a man noted for his true humility, for his interest in education of the masses and, after Wilberforce's death, for succeeding him as leader of the anti-slavery party in the Commons. Forster himself had married in 1850 and built a new house in Burley which he called Wharfeside. He was now Liberal MP for Bradford.

Burley was becoming steadily more industrialised. There were now also the New Mills spinning cotton, a bleach works at Burley-Woodhead and, towards Otley, Ackroyd's worsted mills. However, the construction of the Leeds and Thirsk Railway, completed in 1849, had made comparatively little impact on Lower Wharfedale. Although it crossed the river east of Otley, the nearest station was at Arthington, six and a half miles from the middle of Burley and another four from Ilkley. In 1851, the company had changed its name and became the Leeds Northern Railway and three years later had merged with two others to form the North Eastern. But local people were suspicious of it. Arthington station was less than a mile from the northern mouth of the notorious Bramhope tunnel which had claimed so many navvies' lives. Nor had the bizarre accident of 19th September 1854 faded from memory. That morning, the Parliamentary train from Stockton to Leeds had run into a pile of rubble which had fallen from the roof, three-quarters of the way through the tunnel. The four rear coaches, instead of being derailed, broke free and ran back down the gradient, out of the tunnel and away to the station again before the dazed guard in the rear van, which was of course now leading the charge, was able to stop it. Just as its occupants were recovering their wits and beginning to alight, a fifth carriage full of Irish reapers, minus its front end, came careering down the incline and smashed back-end foremost into the stationary half-train.

Not surprisingly, travellers to and from Burley mostly used the road coaches from Leeds or Bradford, for the omnibus service from Arthington station was in any case a miserable affair. The conveyance of goods, too, was more conveniently and cheaply left to road wagons and vans. It is not difficult to understand how, as head man in Carver's Bradford stables, James heard of the vacancy which had occurred there.

Amongst the new phenomena of the modern age, the only tradition that Burley had to offer of historical interest was its Great Pudding, made and consumed by the inhabitants every seven years. It weighed sixty stones (381kg), half of it in flour and the rest in all manner of fruits. The eating of the Pudding was done opposite the Malt Shovel, a thatched pub at the bottom end of Main Street. At the other end was the Red Lion, a cottage beer-house. Between them stood the Queen's Head with outbuildings, stables and paddocks behind, and this was the place James had found.

The circumstances in which it had become available are important to consider, since they were also those which eventually caused him to leave. The pub had formerly been the property of Sarah Walker, a widow, who in her will dated 13th October 1853, six weeks before she died, left it upon trust to provide an income to help her son James, an agricultural labourer then aged 33, to maintain his three children until the youngest of them reached the age of twenty-one, which would occur in 1873. So in order to provide the income required, it was let to one John Miller. However, he now suddenly died at the age of 42 and his widow Ann had to clear out with her two children, Betty and Fred. Sympathy was

Fig. 8 Sarah Louisa Walker, licensee of the Queen's Head in 1892, was the grand-daughter of the widow Sarah who died in 1853.

not long necessary though, for she soon married William Dalby, a widower of her own age who worked in a stone quarry and had six children of his own. So that solved a problem for her, for him and for all the eight children.

As a fresh reminder of the hazards of steam, a locomotive boiler exploded at Arthington station a month or so after James's move to the Queen's Head. The bang was tremendous and could be heard far up the valley and it was somewhat surprising that only Mary Ann Knowles, aged two, was killed. For James, on the other hand, the railway mania was good fortune. Work was just starting on three new lines – a branch from Arthington to Otley; the Otley and Ilkley Joint Railway, owned by the North Eastern and Midland companies and running through Burley itself; and the Otley and Ilkley Extension Railway, a Midland venture from its Leeds and Bradford line to link with the Otley and Ilkley Joint Railway.

The construction of these lines put every cart, wagon and horse into requisition. James got a horse and cart and took on any haulage job that came his way. With the help of a cheap young girl living in, Mary ran the pub by day and tended her new baby. The pub itself now did a roaring evening trade but it was an anxious time, because the navvies had a particularly bad reputation locally. No one had forgotten the great fight just north of the river when the Leeds and Thirsk line had been under construction. There was no pub at Wescoe Hill, and so the men had organised their own cooperative. Beer at trade rates brought them to the point where they spent more of each day drinking it than working on the line, and the company therefore confiscated all the barrels and locked them up. En masse the navvies stormed the fort, drank every drop of beer and engaged in a bloody battle among themselves in a field of mowing grass. The terrified locals, witnessing a scene that reminded them of the lurid accounts of warfare that they had heard from veterans of Waterloo, could hardly believe, when it was all over, that in the blood-soaked field there was only one man completely dead, lying on a heap of stones. However, James owed a lot to railways. The lack of one had enabled him to find the Queen's Head: and the building of three had provided him with a lucrative haulage business and a pub full of customers.

Early next spring, before the 1864 breeding season began, he acquired his first stallion. From whom he bought it is now impossible to discover, but we do know a little about its pedigree. It had been bred at Frodsham, near Chester, by a man called Whitley. This Whitley had also bred the dam and the grand-dam, and James was able to find out particulars of all the sires, and approved them. He looked at the horse from every angle, tested it and ran his hand over every bone in its legs. It was a black horse and a good one, and he could get it at a reasonable price because, now rising four, it had yet to make its reputation as a sire. He went home, thought about it and decided to take the plunge. The Forshaw savings were kept in what he and his wife called "the old stocking". Next morning, this was emptied of most of its contents, and James made a little speech to Mary Ann, promising her that one day he would be famous all over the world for his stallions. Then he set off, and returned triumphantly in the evening.

He called his horse Matchless, and prepared him for the season. Up and down the dale, but mostly down, where there were more mares, he travelled him on daily outings from home. It is doubtful whether any horse ever had more attention lavished upon him or was presented in more immaculate condition, or whether any young man in charge of a stallion ever made a greater impression on potential customers. They looked at him with a mixture of respect and bewilderment, for he was most particular about everything and yet at the same time most obliging. By the end of the season, he had had a lot of customers. Matchless was still in good hard condition and full of spirits, and James immediately set to work to prepare him for the local summer shows. To succeed anywhere in these during the Sixties, a horse had to be made fat and shiny, but if he wanted to win and increase his reputation, he had to accept the risks associated with the continuance of high feeding after sudden cessation of sexual and pedestrian activity. So he exercised him assiduously and won several prizes. These enabled him to sell the horse for more than he had paid in the first place and also saved the cost of keeping him through the following eight months.

His 1865 horse was of the same age as Matchless – now therefore five years old, and was really a better one. Bred in Staffordshire, it was the old traditional colour of that county, a whole brown with not white hair upon it. Its antecedents included horses owned by that celebrity of an earlier age, John Chadwick himself. James called him Brown Stout, after one of the remembered horses at Dutch Barn Farm. Perhaps his thoughts about his father were mellowing, for when Mary had her third child on 5th July, as a second successful travelling season was coming to an end, he was given the name Tom. The mother was particular to notice that, at about the age of three weeks, the child twitched his ears whenever Brown Stout passed the room where he lay. James said this was a sign that he would become a true horseman.

On 1st August, the Otley and Ilkley Joint Railway and the Otley and Ilkley Extension Railway were both opened to passenger traffic. One could go to Ilkley by NER or by MR in about twelve minutes, choosing from 14 trains daily. In the opposite direction, there were five daily trains to Leeds and five to Bradford. Coming home, you started from Bradford at exactly the same moment as someone else started from Leeds, but ended up in different parts of the same train, which everyone considered a most remarkable thing. The significance of all this was not lost on James. On request, a horse box could be attached to the rear end of any passenger train. If he had a lot of stallions, he could send them out pretty well anywhere in England – and they would arrive in a day! Another thing was that they were beginning these days to set up wires for the electric telegraph alongside the railway lines. When he became a proprietor of many stallions, he could contact his men and they could contact him. If a stallion, hundreds of miles away, broke down or fell sick or was injured, he could be informed at once and could get a substitute off to arrive within twenty-four hours. James loved to peer into the future and make grand plans for it – but meanwhile he only had Brown Stout.

The next year, while at Otley 'clearing up' mares at the end of his second season, the horse fell dead. James was thankful he had had the good sense to dip into the very bottom of the stocking in order to take out insurance. But when he discovered that the company had not only stopped payments but had closed down, he was really in trouble. He could see no hope of buying a replacement. Now that the railways had been completed, the apparently limitless opportunities for cartage work had dwindled to almost nothing. He was intending just to do coal deliveries during the winter months, and the Queen's Head was no longer full of thirsty navvies in the evenings. However, Manny Gant came to the rescue. The Gants – Emmanuel at Bilsby Field near Alford in the Lincoln Marsh and William nearby at Thurlby – were well-established and considerable stallion men and Manny's first impulse, whenever he heard of anyone in trouble, was to go and help him. This is how the roan five-year-old Thumper, bred near Ely, came to Burley the following spring. In later years James often said that, if the time ever came when Mr Gant needed a good turn, he hoped to be there to do it. Sadly the time did come and the turn was very amply done.

The next Forshaw infant, Richard, was born on 16th July 1868. Thumper had finished his second profitable season and brought his tally of prizes over two years to twelve. Then along came a buyer from Germany and James was firmly on his feet again.

One of Thumper's last mares had been an aging local one called Diamond, which had never bred anything much. She belonged to William Walker of Mount Stead, a moor-side holding of 125 acres between Burley village and Ben Rydding. This was a real family farm, staffed by William's teenage sons. His wife Elizabeth had her daughter Rebecca to help in the house and her own sister, Ellen Buckle, at 61 thirteen years older than herself, to act as dairy maid. Her husband's relationship to James's landlords, if any, is doubtful, for there were a lot of Walkers in Burley.

Diamond's colt foal the next spring was a very good one. James, with more money in his pocket now, offered considerably more for it than anybody else could be expected to give. The delighted Walker told everyone of the superb foal he had got by that young Forshaw's horse out of his old mare. Though a prophet rarely is honoured at home, the publican at the Queen's Head was now recognised as the most remarkable judge of a good foal when he saw one and as a true gentleman who did not haggle about the price – a man anyone could do business with. As for James, this was the first of hundreds of such deals. His maxim was "Look to the mare". And he knew about Diamond. She was not much to look at now, old and work-weary and in rough condition, but she had quality. As for the foal, he would have to wait and see how it developed. Meanwhile, Thumper's replacement for 1869 was the nine-year-old chestnut Oxford, bred only fourteen miles away and not far from the southern bank of the Wharfe on its passage to Wetherby.

By the autumn, James was in a stronger financial position than he had ever been and spent less time carting coal and more of it buying and selling colts, fillies and mares, though he always had a customer in view before he bought. He was now even able occasionally to indulge his inclination towards anything which would give him a laugh, a trait not inherited from his father. He competed, for example, in the Wharfedale Races, held on 19th October, a Tuesday. The Farmers' Stakes of ten sovereigns, for full-aged horses to carry twelve stones, was run at 3.30 over three-quarters of a mile. Five lined up for this, and J Forshaw was on Eclipse. This animal failed to live up to its name but managed to finish fifth. This qualified him to take part in the two-mile Consolation Stakes of five sovereigns for losers an hour later, but there is no record of his performance in that.

At about this time, he acquired the brown Nonsuch, another nine-year-old. This animal had won two good prizes but, becoming intractable, had disillusioned more than one owner. He was now in poor condition and James bought him for a song. He had a feeling that the horse had suffered more from mismanagement than anything else. He worked hard on him and when he brought him out at shows the next year, he took first prize every time, including the Yorkshire itself. Within two years, he had made Nonsuch into a northern celebrity. By the end of the 1872 season this horse's show rewards totalled almost exactly £400 – all in first prizes except for the one occasion when he was beaten into second place and paradoxically achieved instant national fame as a result.

To recognise the significance of what happened, it is necessary to retreat three years to the autumn of 1869, when James first bought the horse. That was the year when the third Earl of Ellesmere at the age of 22 became the first man, other than Bakewell, to set up a stud of English cart horses "for the express purpose" (if one may quote oneself) of "breeding them on scientific principles of pedigree and conformation". Though James Forshaw was in fact a potentially better man at this than either the Earl or even than his manager Henry Heaton, his lordship had a certain natural advantage over him. His Worsley Hall estate near Manchester extended to about 13,300 acres, beneath which he had the additional benefit of forty-two miles of subterranean canals on four levels, all carrying coal from his mines and adding to his wealth. With these resources, he was able to spare a thousand acres for his scientific stud farm, upon which he erected more than a hundred carefully planned horse boxes together with all the ancillary buildings that efficiency required. James's rented pub and hand-to-mouth income, which was at peril if he tried to experiment, could scarcely match this.

Lord Ellesmere's example was quickly followed by a triumvirate, also in Lancashire, which approached the matter in a different way. Its leader was Thomas Horrocks Miller, whose wealth came from several cotton mills and who owned the Singleton Park estate, a few miles from Blackpool. Three years older than the Earl and four years younger than James Forshaw, he was enthusiastically supported by his vicar the Rev Leonard Wood who, at fifty, was twice his age. The third member was none other than Thomas Townley Townley-Parker who as a young man had seen Thomas Forshaw's stallions when he rode over from Cuerdon Hall to visit his aged grandmother at Astley Hall. They too began in 1869, by forming a group to encourage light horse breeding. However, Parson Wood suggested that they could do more for farmers by raising the quality of cart horses instead. So they set up the Fylde Cart Horse Breeding Improvement Company. Whereas the Earl aimed to produce the finest individual specimens, free from every hereditary defect, which would be dispersed by sale to all parts of the country, the Fylde Company's objective was simply to purchase the best possible stallions and persuade the local farmers to use them. Their second horse, acquired from Norfolk in the autumn of 1871, was the most famous stallion in England, William Welcher's Honest Tom. He was still only six years old, but had won first prize at the Royal Show for five years in succession. It is difficult now to appreciate such glamour. Anyone who took the slightest interest in agricultural affairs, all town horsemen and owners such as the manager of Carver's and everyone who read the papers would know who won the Royal. Honest Tom had already covered enough mares to make the mind reel but, still in the prime of life, was eager and willing to transform the cart horses of the Fylde.

Messrs Miller, Wood and Townley-Parker exhibited him once again at the 1872 Royal, and again he won first prize. He was clearly unbeatable. They showed him also at the Nottinghamshire Show, which most people thought was unfair on the county men. James Forshaw also exhibited Nonsuch. The judge began by placing Honest Tom in his usual position, with Nonsuch second to him. Later, after the close individual inspection, he astounded everyone by sending all the horses out of the ring, and following them. He came back again accompanied by the co-judge with whom he was alternating in the classes and they were followed by Honest Tom and Nonsuch. The two men looked at them, made them walk and trot again, felt them, talked between themselves, and sent them out. They then produced a referee to help them and the two animals were summoned a third time. The final verdict went in favour of Honest Tom. Perhaps that was inevitable. The referee was not fool enough to become the first man in England not to place Honest Tom first – especially at a mere county show.

Everyone on the show-ground who fancied his knowledge of horses joined the queues to judge both animals privately afterwards and, according to press reports, ninety per cent of them thought Nonsuch should have won. Whether their view was coloured by a natural desire to support the under-horse, it is difficult to say, but it all helped James to achieve fame throughout England which was almost as great as it would have been if he had actually won. He capitalised on his glory by selling Nonsuch for £400 to an American called Reilly. Honest Tom had cost the triumvirate £500, which was then easily a record, so far as can be discovered, for a cart horse. But Nonsuch was now twelve, twice the age that Honest Tom had been then, so the price was amazing. The émigré, aided by the story that went with him, caused such a stir that James began to receive letters both from the United States and Canada, enquiring if he could find them any more horses of that calibre. He saw this as a great opportunity, but resolved to wait until he could get exactly what was required. He was anxious to build a lasting reputation rather than to make a fast and temporary buck.

For a year or two now, he had been able to keep and travel more than one stallion at a time, paying a groom to take the second. There was the bulky bay Waggon Shaker, and the brown Wellington. There was Columbus, out of a mare by his father's well-remembered Short Legs. He exported this one, after a year, to someone in Italy. There was Waxwork, bred by Willy Gant. This was a fine animal, typical of the Fens in weight, and without blemish. In the spring of 1873, at the age of six, it was dispatched to America to confirm the impression that Mr James Forshaw was a man to do business with. Another horse was sent that year to Russia, but its name, if it ever had one, is lost, and so is that of the purchaser.

That autumn Mary Ann gave birth for the sixth time. James Dagger had died in 1867 at the age of four, but Tom was now eight, Mary Ann junior six, Richard five and Agnes (the future collector of her father's biographical scraps) nearly three. The new baby was a substitute James. Margaret, still in Lancashire, was twelve. Tom was already going to the school founded by Mr Fison and Mr Forster. The latter's interest in education was now on a broader front. In Mr Gladstone's first premiership it had fallen to him as Vice-President of the Privy Council to introduce the Elementary Education Bill in the February of 1870 – as a result of which his name remains familiar today, when those of some Prime Ministers cannot be recalled by many people. In this year of 1873, he had attempted to strengthen the Act by making universal education compulsory, but this was met by failure, even though it was to be only temporary.

By now James was under notice to quit the Queen's Head. Earlier in the year, James Fawcett Walker, the youngest of the three grandsons named in Widow Walker's will of 1853, had come of age and so he and his brothers were entitled to demand of their father that he should hand over the property to them. However, the two older ones, Robert and Jeremiah, were stonemasons and James, like the father, an agricultural labourer, and the three were quite happy as they were (There were in addition four younger children, but they had been born too late to qualify for a share in the pub, and so it did not matter what they thought). On 5th March, the three signed an indenture which "in consideration of the natural love and affection which they the said Robert Walker Jeremiah Walker and James Fawcett Walker have for their father the said James Walker" conveyed the beneficial ownership to him. He could do what he liked with it – except that "in case any woman shall at any time hereafter become his widow such widow shall not be entitled to dower in or out of the said messuage or dwelling-house hereditaments and premises". As he had never remarried after losing his wife and therefore could not have a widow, he was not bothered by this. He was now 53 and it would be better to draw quarts and pints than to labour in the fields.

4. The Angel at Blyth

Mrs Mary Walker of Blyth Hall near the northwestern boundary of Nottingham-shire was in no way related to William Walker, owner of the aged Diamond or to James Walker, now of the Queen's Head. She was very rich, owning all Blyth's 2373 acres. Her new tenant at the Angel, James Forshaw, was lucky to have so easily found just the sort of place he needed. It had stabling, now mostly unused because of the railways, for two hundred horses and there were several good paddocks behind. She too was fortunate. Who else would want such a large inn, now that few travellers came that way? And, as for quenching the local thirst, were there not more than enough pubs competing for that trade?

When Mary Ann Forshaw looked from any of the front windows of her new home, she saw, across the road, the great church of St Mary and St Martin. This was very fitting, for the Angel had been built, on the very edge of Sherwood Forest, to accommodate the masons who were building that Benedictine Priory founded by Roger de Builli in 1088. This was one of the earliest of the great Norman monastic houses in England, old-fashioned even when it was new, for in plan and rough workmanship it resembled the abbey churches built in Normandy a generation or so before the Conqueror arrived in England. When completed, it was dedicated to St Mary the Virgin. And now, to appreciate the situation of Mary the widow and Mary the stallion-man's wife in the context of 1873, it is probably helpful to glance at one or two events in the history of the church and inn at Blyth.

In 1217, when one of the greatest of the early tournaments was held on the tilting-ground north of the township, the Angel was packed with people as was every hostelry for miles around. A little later, the King's licence became necessary to hold these popular contests, and there was sometimes a difficulty. For example, just as a tournament was about to begin on 2nd November 1273, the Prior was put in the embarrassing position of having to stand up on the field before a large assembly of the aristocracy and a mass of common spectators and read a letter from Edward I forbidding the event. Somewhat thoughtlessly, his Majesty himself came to Blyth the very next year to lead a team against the Burgundians, captained by le Comte de Chalon. The ceremonies were courtly, but the tournament itself became bad-tempered and needed a stronger referee. In the same year Robert de Insula, the newly consecrated Bishop of Durham, stayed a night at the Angel on his way to see the King. At this period, the Priory was not particularly popular, because it owned the whole of Blyth township and was steadily increasing the dues at its four toll-bars for everything passing through.

About 1290, the south aisle of the church was removed and a new wider one built, as great as the mighty nave, to provide a place of worship for the

Fig. 9 The early Norman nave
of the Priory Church at Blyth,
founded in 1088 by Roger de Builli.

Fig. 10 The Angel wears more or less the same face as in James Forshaw's time.

people. Something like a century later, this secular part of the building was completely cut off from the other by filling in the arches. It was dedicated separately to St Martin, who is presumed to have been the patron saint of the tiny Saxon church which had stood there until 1088.

After the Priory was dissolved in 1535, most of the conventual buildings were dismantled and Blyth Hall was built on the foundations of the cloister and refectory. The great church itself presented as it does today the odd appearance of having twin naves, the one a parish church and the other empty. Though the establishment in honour of the Virgin lasted a mere 447 years, her name has remained associated with that of St Martin in the longer period that the place has been simply an enormous parish church in a little township. The lands passed through several owners until their purchase by John Mellish in 1635 and in 1738 his descendant acquired also the manorial rights of nearby Hodsock. The Mellishes made a modern village out of ancient Blyth, which is why the Angel, when James came there, no longer looked mediaeval, but wore a decent 18th-century dress.

It had long been claimed that Blyth acquired its name from the mirth and general good fellowship of the inhabitants, and the Mellish family did much to keep this going. The one fly in the ointment of life was actually a beetle – the may-bug, brown-clock, dorr-beetle or cockchafer. This large and destructive armour-plated flying pest was so numerous in the parish that people had to be paid, at three pence a peck, to destroy it. In 1788, 3743 pecks – 7486 gallons or over 34,000 litres – were harvested and £47.1.2d was paid out (This appears to be 5s 5d, or roughly £0.27, too much). No statistic is available for the average number of may-bugs in a peck but it must have been considerable.

Unfortunately, Colonel Henry Francis Mellish, a famous dandy, gambled away the whole of Blyth in 1805 and retired to Hodsock. There is a story that he had actually lost all his properties, but managed to win Hodsock back at a louse race in which he surreptitiously used a hot plate for his entry to run across whereas his opponent had only a cold one. Blyth, however, was sold to Joshua Walker, a partner in a family cast-iron manufactory on the outskirts of Rotherham and it was his grandson's widow whose tenant and neighbour James had now become.

Sherwood had long since receded over the horizon and shrunk to almost nothing. Blyth, though well-wooded still, was open, low-lying and flat, drained by a network of streams and dykes into the Ryton river, which encompassed it on three sides as it meandered towards its confluence with the Idle and eventually the Trent. The long-thriving cottage industry of basket-making still flourished. May-bugs were under control and the chief bane of Blyth was now Mrs Walker herself. Unlike the genial Mellishes, who were still at Hodsock, she behaved very grandly. For example, when she went to church, the great west door was opened specially for her and as she sailed stately eastwards to her elevated pew she was preceded by a footman bearing a heated cushion on which she could lower her elderly buttocks.

She was also very stingy. Her meanness was so grinding as to be

Fig. 11 Henry Francis Mellish, whose follies forced him to sell Blyth to Joshua Walker.

commemorated by her wretched servants in a ballad called 'Fair Evelyn the Pride of Pork Hall' – a sensible use of pseudonyms. Its sixteen verses become tedious and so the first four and the last will suffice here:

In a neat little village in fair Nottinghamshire
There lives a blooming damsel, as you shall quickly hear.
She is not very young, though handsome and tall.
Her name is Fair Evelyn, the pride of Pork Hall.

Pork Hall, I am informed, was a place of renown
Where peace and plenty and every good thing did abound
In days gone by before the Squire did fall,
But it is now much changed by the pride of Pork Hall.

If you are a servant and come to live at this place,
Misery and starvation stare you in the face.
Our food is all weighed, and measured the coal.
Everything is locked up by the pride of Pork Hall.

The cattle of this woman all share the same fate.
The hay is all weighed that the cows and horses do eat.
The pigs eat the droppings that from the horses do fall,
So now you know the reason why we call it Pork Hall....

So pluck up your spirits and an effort let us make
To restore this little village to its once happy state.
We once more might be happy if the Devil would call
And fetch away Evelyn, the pride of Pork Hall.

When he moved into the Angel, James had plenty to do – without any assistance from the Hall – in repairing the stables and converting the two hundred stalls into a much smaller number of loose boxes. He now had six stallions and to celebrate the move renamed Diamond's son Robin Hood. He also had the brown Lincolnshire Hero (bred at Wilburton in Cambridgeshire) and three four-year-olds. Waggon Shaker, his second of that name, hailed from Yorkshire, as did John Bull III, whose previous owners were somewhat vague about the name and address of his breeder, which they gave as "Dook, The Levels, Yorkshire". Paragon Tom had won the cup as a foal at Boston, where he was born but had not grown into a show horse. However, his legs and feet were good and his virility so impressive that he looked like becoming a moneyspinner if James could persuade people what he could do for mares whose own limbs were not of the best. A three-year-old was showing no sexual enthusiasm, and so was castrated and sold. There was also now a colt from Lincolnshire which he called Young Blyth and a yearling, bred locally. He called this one Dan Howsin as a memorial to the man who for forty years had been the best stallion-proprietor in Nottinghamshire, or perhaps all England. In 1843 Dan had won the only two prizes, 'Agricultural' and 'Dray', offered at the fifth Royal Show, held at Derby. No one else had ever done that. He had now passed on, but it was his Drayman and Champion that had sired the dam and grand-dam of the horse now called after him.

In his second season at Blyth, James took Lincolnshire Hero to the stallion show organised by the Winterton Association, and won the hundred pounds premium. This meant that he had to give an undertaking that the horse would be available in that part of North Lincolnshire for three months to serve members' mares at a very small fixed fee. The larger part of the prize was to be withheld until the season had been completed.

The thinking of those who formed such associations as the Winterton was imaginative and progressive, but the system was not in practice satisfactory. Unsuccessful candidates wasted their time and money. There might be another show a few days later, perhaps fifty or a hundred miles distant. If they tried and failed again there, it might then be too late to plan a profitable route for the horse. Consequently, such events frequently failed to attract the class of stallion that members hoped for, or even to produce anything better than was already in their district. And then, during the season, there was usually a row of some kind about a premium horse.

Let us hear the sort of complaints members made: the groom failed to follow the route properly and missed out stopping places; mares belonging to non-members were being served at the same fee as members' mares; what right did the groom have to refuse mares, as he had done three times? That time the horse was kicked, the groom had been careless – and the substitute had arrived too late and was inferior; on Saturdays, the groom was always so drunk that he couldn't get the mares done in time; Mr Smith was offered the horse for an extra mare at only five shillings if the book wasn't signed; the groom had been caught having sexual relations under a haystack with Mr Robinson's dairy maid; the horse had not done well at all and some of the premium would be withheld.

Hear now the owner's and groom's point of view: the route was impossible to adhere to or, if it wasn't, members kept asking for detours to suit themselves; many of the mares brought to the horse were not ready, or they were too thin, or too fat; that time his penis was kicked, no one had warned the man that she'd done it before; to complain about the substitute was intolerable – members were too ignorant to recognise quality when they saw it; when the groom refused to try mares it was because they were unclean: he ought to be thanked for being so alert – otherwise the infection would have been spread; on Saturdays, the mare owners were more drunk than he was, and he could not get on with the business; he had been reprimanded for his offer to Mr Smith, but had only made it out of sympathy for the poor old fool – what about Mr Jones, who tried to bribe the man with a three month's supply of tobacco? As for the dairy maid, Mrs Robinson, if she had had any sense, would have locked her up when the horse was about, to stop her throwing herself at a respectable married man with three children – and while on that subject, what about Mr Clark's slut of a sister last year, thirty if she was a day, seducing a groom scarcely out of his teens? Mares were fewer than had been promised and their poor quality and condition would damage the reputation of a valuable horse.

No association had any link with any other, and each consequently had to learn from its own mistakes. So did the stallion-owner. There was no society of any kind to which either might turn for help or advice. It is not surprising that the number of premium associations remained few and that most cart stallions were still travelled on speculation.

In the autumn of 1875, the year he won the Winterton premium, James acquired a two-year-old which most men would not have looked at twice. It had been bred only ten miles away, at Sturton-le-Steeple. Tom, a pupil at the village school and a chorister at the Priory church, was now ten, and saw the animal arrive. It was "a tall, leggy, heavy-limbed colt with wide feet, good pasterns and broad legs growing a mass of long hair." It was in wretched condition and not beautiful. Tom asked his father why he had bought such a thing. James explained. It had all the desirable points and no bad ones. He told the boy to watch it develop over the next few years, and he would learn something. He was going to call it What's Wanted.

The business was growing rapidly and he needed extra land. So he applied to Mrs Walker and got the tenancy of the vacant Mill Farm, where the water-driven mill was useful in preparing feed. The sort of tenant who rejoiced the old dame's heart, he was now employing five or six full-time men, but each year he needed more stallion-leaders. Leading was only a seasonal job, but plenty of men did other work at other times of the year. Nor was there any shortage of capable sons of small farmers who were glad to release them for high pay. The best man of all was the one who was likely to be available for some years to come. If regularly sent to the same district, he would become a trusted agent, welcomed back as an old friend the following spring by customers and, in the search for good foals to buy in or other young stock for selling on, he would become James's eyes and ears in distant parts.

Most people equated excellence with enormous weight and power, but no horse weighing a ton would ever have come into existence without artificial selection. Selection simply for size and strength accentuated any existing detrimental characteristics and where defects were not bred out, they were becoming inbred. In the 1870s, the vast majority of heavy geldings, arriving at the age of five to begin their town career, lasted no more than four years before something incapacitated them. Horses had not evolved on hard unyielding roads or in stinking town air and fog. They had to be sound in wind and limb to withstand them and to survive gross over-working, badly ventilated stables and, frequently, positive cruelty, all of which disgraced England in the 1870s. Uniquely perhaps among stallion owners, James had had four years' first-hand experience of the situation in towns. Carver's had hundreds of horses and they were the best obtainable, but he also saw the worst on the streets of Manchester and Bradford. He knew everything that could be wrong, or go wrong, with a town horse.

Most defects were of the leg. Deficiency of good bone below the knee – soft rounded bones instead of flat and hard ones – fleshiness of the lower leg conducive to the growth of coarse and curly hair, which in turn led to the disgusting and eventually incapacitating condition known as grease – pasterns which were too short or too upright, or both – narrow feet – all these things were a matter of heredity. One could see them in the young animal. Other evils were more subtle. If in the adult horse the cartilages of the pedal bone hardened and eventually actually ossified, it had a sidebone. If, instead, an entirely new growth developed on one of the bones below the fetlock, there was a ringbone. An enlargement of bone developing on the inside of the hock was a bone spavin. These three developments, hastened by poor conformation and hard pavements, led to lameness.

Nervous diseases were also insidious. An adult horse might start to twitch the muscles of its hind legs and refuse, or be unable, to back a vehicle. It had become a shiverer. Another horse, with an involuntary snatching up of its hind leg, had developed stringhalt. Diseases of the respiratory system, too, developed with age. Foals were not born roaring or whistling any more than they came into the world shivering or snatching their little legs, or equipped with a pair of baby sidebones, ringbones or spavins, but if either of their parents had one or more of these afflictions, it was likely that they also would eventually suffer – and the quickest way of finding out was to sell them into town. To complete the catalogue, cataract, or propensity towards cataract, appeared to be hereditary.

It would be absurd to suggest that James was the only man in England with brains enough to understand the position and to know what was needed. The problem was simply that, since about 1840, English farming had steadily grown so prosperous, that the advantages of breeding better cart horses did not generally attract people of intelligence – they concentrated upon the more profitable products of the farm. Few scientific agriculturalists or stockbreeders, scarcely any improving landlord, had given the cart horse much thought. The tenant farmers, who bred them, got their price for the foals, and were satisfied, for they did not know a better price. Industry, commerce, the cartage men and the railways paid for the adult product. There was no link between the two. The farmer's sole partner was the stallion-owner – often an ignorant man himself, the owner of just one or two horses.

The improvement of cattle by the use of certain selected sires, to which much attention had been given, could be proved quite simply. By acquiring a succession of good bulls a man could transform his herd. He was independent of his neighbours or of anyone else. The men who bred a cart foal or two every year could not hope for improvement as long as they were dependent on stallions whose power to transmit soundness or unsoundness had not really been considered. What is worse, even when a good-looking foal grew up sound, they could not be fully aware of it. If a colt, it left them at six months and they never heard where it ended up. If a mare, it stayed at home and was never put to the supreme test of the towns.

The few men who did appreciate James's point of view were not, generally speaking, themselves breeders. One such was Professor W C Spooner of the Royal Veterinary College, who as far back as 1861 had created something of a sensation at the Royal Show. He and his team of inspectors had to check all animal exhibits on arrival, in order to prevent or curtail the spread of infectious diseases. But he did more than that. He reported all the worst cases of roaring and sidebone among the cart horses. The judges, who would normally have ignored these points as their predecessors had always done, were compelled to take some notice. Thanks to Spooner's influence, a second inspection, for hereditary unsoundness, was instituted at the next Show. However, his system lasted only eight years, after which the senior horse steward reported with some relief the restoration of the status quo. The special inspection, he said, had caused exhibitors to be so nervous of their reputations that many even of the best horses in the country were no longer sent to the Royal, with the result that the numbers exhibited in these classes were so few as to be "a disgrace to a national society". Few practical men would have supported James Forshaw – and he was only the landlord of the Angel at Blyth – in his belief that it was a greater disgrace when the show ring, and the prize list too, was filled with roaring and sidebones.

5. Pedigree, Peers and Show

By the end of the 1860s, there were pedigree registers for four breeds of cattle. The Seventies saw an acceleration of this movement and before the decade was out the number of herd books had reached double figures. Except for the General Stud Book, dating back to the previous century and catering only for Thoroughbreds, there was no register for any kind of horse until the Earl of Dunmore in the spring of 1877 persuaded fellow Scotsmen to establish a pedigree society for the Clydesdale. Although this was indeed an ancient breed, its transformation into a true heavy draught horse had been achieved by importing great numbers of stallions and mares from Derbyshire and other midland counties. Consequently, English breeders were infuriated by the march which his Lordship had stolen on them. Supporters of the Suffolk horse were the first to react to the Scottish challenge – and reasonably so, for their breed was by far the purest of the three. They held a meeting in the Town Hall at Ipswich on 19th June the same year and founded the Suffolk Horse Society.

It was that energetic cricketing, racing, shooting enthusiast and novelist, the Earl of Ellesmere who got the rest of England going. On 13th February the next year at the first of what he called his "weeding out sales" when forty-five of his surplus horses fetched £6184.50, he literally buttonholed Frederic Street from Somersham in Huntingdonshire and asked him to take the initiative. Fred was due to read a paper on the breeding of draught horses at the Farmers' Club in London three weeks later, so he put a proposal before the members and an open meeting was called for 1st April 1878, when the English Cart Horse Society was founded. The only concession to the date was the absurd title: but, now that 'Black' was out of the question, because most of the horses were bay, grey or even parti-coloured, no one could think of a better one. The Earl was elected President. The Hon Edward Coke (whose father the first Earl of Leicester is better remembered as "Coke of Norfolk", the populariser of scientific farming) was appointed chairman of a committee to produce a stud book.

When the Prince of Wales, who until then had bred only Clydesdales as did his mother at Windsor, agreed to become Patron of the new society, its success was assured. There was a stampede of nobility and gentry, led by Earl Spencer and the Earl of Powis, with the Dukes of Devonshire, Bedford, Marlborough and Westminster not far behind, each offering a guinea to join or ten to be a member for life. The Earl of Dunmore also joined, but only as a spy, as did Herman Biddell, joint founder of the Suffolk Horse Society. If Mary Ann, who had recently completed her childbearing with the birth and death of a baby girl and the birth of little William, retained any lingering doubts about the propriety of being married to a stallion-owner, these quickly evaporated.

James was soon spending whole weeks at a time travelling to hunt up the

Fig. 12 Francis Granville Egerton was fifteen when he succeeded his father as 3rd Earl of Ellesmere, thirty when he set the English Cart Horse Society in motion and over sixty at the time of this picture.

pedigrees of past stallions. Other volunteers in this activity were men of leisure, but he had to make time for it. Then he had to sort out and check his notes. "Many and many a morning" he later told his daughter Agnes, "I found myself at two and three o'clock still at my desk. I could foresee a great future before our breed of horse and I thought that, by giving as much help as possible in this critical time of the Society's infancy, I could assist to put it on such a foundation as never to look behind again. The pedigree system, if only the farmers adopted it, would produce a better horse. And a good horse takes no more keeping than a bad one."

He combined his researches with the constant hunt for promising colts. His export business had recently grown, with the sudden boom in the American market, to an astonishing size. In some periods of the year, he was almost perpetually travelling, for he tried always to maintain the reputation he had been building for good, hard-wearing animals. Most stallions sent to America were of the second grade: but he regarded that as short-sighted folly.

Those train journeys were wearisome, especially coming home at night. Ranskill station was two and a half miles from the Angel door. It was on the main line, but no express called there. So he had to alight at Retford and take the little stopping train. The boredom of travel sometimes prompted the bubbling but somewhat odd sense of humour which he displayed when the fancy took him. He once noticed a man in a corner seat who had a very red nose. So he leaned over and pretended to light his cigar at it. The stranger reacted predictably and began to lay into him. After a brief struggle, they settled down amicably enough, for James was essentially a friendly man who meant no harm. He drank little and rarely, partly because in his line of business social drinking was difficult to keep within bounds. He was meeting people all day long. And he had, too, an object lesson against inebriation in his brother George whom he had taken into his protection and brought over to Blyth. Poor alcoholic George worked for him as a labourer in a spasmodic way.

A spring show of stallions used to be held in Birmingham at the Bingley Hall, and in 1879 this became a sort of unofficial championship contest for members of the new breed society. James entered What's Wanted, which had developed from the leggy colt of four years before into an almost perfect six-year-old. For three years, he had been devoted exclusively to Lancashire mares, the previous season as winner of the £100 Blackpool premium. At Birmingham he won his class. James's other exhibit, Temptation, was also first, amongst the three-year-olds. Then What's Wanted was awarded the gold plate as the best stallion in the show. Years later, people would ask James what was the finest horse he ever owned and he would always reply, "Let alone owned, What's Wanted was the best horse I ever saw".

Tom, who had been puzzled by What's Wanted as a two-year-old, was now getting on for fourteen and in May had his first experience of exhibiting a horse on his own. He took a two-year-old filly called Maggie to Newark Show, where success would enhance her value in the eyes of whatever customer his father had in mind. In steady rain, she won first prize, but she had to appear in the grand parade the next day in order to receive it. So he walked her to the Newark Arms for the night. The following morning, it was still raining, but much harder. On the way up Appletongate, he met a stranger who said "I wouldn't go if I were you, sonny. Not a soul going." Tom looked at the water streaming down Maggie's legs, turned her round and caught the next train to Ranskill. The prize money arrived by post, which was a relief, because he had been wondering whether he had done right. That summer of 1879, the worst in living memory, was symbolic of the deep depression now beginning to sweep over British farming – a depression that, ironically, affected every form of farm produce except heavy cart horses, which in the good times had had no thought expended on their breeding. Their value when ready for town work, especially if manifestly sound and durable, was rising fast.

The Council of the English Cart Horse Society decided at a meeting on 9th December that they ought to hold a breed show, something that the Clydesdale and Suffolk Societies never contemplated. Victorians were not in the habit of dawdling about and so the doors of the Agricultural Hall at Islington opened just under twelve weeks later, on 2nd March. James, who brought Tom with him, had decided not to exhibit What's Wanted or any others because he did not think it right to push them from their rough winter state into show condition at such short notice. Others may have felt the same, for only 114 horses arrived. Over forty were thrown out again by Professor Pritchard whose duty as Veterinary Inspector was to disqualify any animal he considered to have any of the serious hereditary faults.

The arrival of the Prince and Princess of Wales with their three daughters on the second day set the seal on the sudden gentility now attaching to the breeding of animals whose function was to pull refuse carts, timber carriages and all industrial England's heavy loads. It was fitting that, when his Royal Highness presented the champion stallion cup, the recipient was the Earl of Ellesmere, whose Admiral had been bred by John Milner, a small farmer in the Fylde.

Topsy, the champion mare, was exhibited by the famous Scotsman Lawrence Drew. Three years before, she had won first prize at Glasgow as a Clydesdale, and she had already had two foals by Drew's own outstanding Clydesdale stallion Prince of Wales. But she herself was a true old-fashioned Black of purest Derbyshire descent. Mr Drew was a popular visitor at this London Show because everyone knew that, with some hundreds of his supporters, he had refused to join the Clydesdale Society on the ground that the English and Scottish draught horses were really the same breed. He had now proved his point. So he sold Topsy to T H Miller. She went into the Fylde and he went home to Hamilton where he set about forming another new society in opposition to that of the Earl of Dunmore.

During that show, the first volume of the new stud book – 744 pages of it – was ready for distribution, thanks to frantic efforts by the printers and binders, Cassell, Petter and Galpin. Members could pick up their copies free, but others had to pay half a guinea. It contained the pedigrees of 2381 stallions (mares would have to wait until Volume 2), arranged in alphabetical order and numbered accordingly. Stallion no 1 was a horse called A1, foaled in 1864. The last was Yorkshire Stingo 2381, a year younger. In date, the earliest was Blaze 183, bred in 1770, and the latest were 653 horses foaled in the ten years 1867-1876. Six were credited to 'Thomas Forshaw, The Market Place, Chorley'. Persisting in his unaccountable reluctance to admit the existence of Dutch Barn Farm, James had supported their claim to inclusion by sending Mr Coke the advertisement cards which he had kept as his only mementos of boyhood. Kirby was in because, though sold into Russia, he had first begotten plenty of offspring at home. Lord Nelson and Short Legs failed to qualify. Sixteen of his own horses were included and only nine people, dead or alive, were listed with more. Naturally, figures do not do justice to the great men of early times because so many of their horses were difficult to evaluate or even identify. Nevertheless, twenty-four of John Chadwick's stallions were in.

At the second London Show in 1881, James won third prize among the senior stallions (five years old and upwards) with Temptation, but his great achievement, unrecognised because few knew the story behind it, was with Bar None. Only eight months earlier this horse, then a three-year-old, had been working on a farm near Doncaster – uncastrated only because of his owner's

Fig. 13 This representation of Bar None is somewhat stylised, the artist over-emphasising the shortness of his legs.

idle habits. Walter Johnson of Hatfield spotted him from over a hedge, bought him and sold him on to James, who effected such a transformation that he now won fourth prize in the four-year-old class. Soon afterwards, some person now unknown wrote an enthusiastic letter to Richard Graham, an émigré Scotsman who "wired from Canada asking my lowest price for him", as James later told someone. "I wired back, and he accepted. Then the horse lamed himself. I wired to Canada, but Graham had already sailed. When he got to my place, he stripped himself and bathed that horse for sixteen hours a day for three days, he was so anxious to have him. He came to the conclusion, however, that he couldn't get him strong enough to meet the Atlantic. This was the best thing that ever happened to me."

Next year, the judges made Bar None supreme champion of the Show and James was immediately offered £1,400 for him – then a fantastic price. Less than twenty-four hours earlier he had arranged to let him for the season to the Ellesmere Entire Horse Society. The agreement was so far only a verbal one and the would-be purchaser might have been willing to take the horse subject to the three months' hire, but the deputation from Shropshire refused to countenance any change of ownership. They considered they were also hiring Mr Forshaw's expertise – so there was no sale.

Local societies of this sort were now beginning to supersede the premium-awarding clubs. Some of them bought a stallion, but this practice was soon to be shown as potentially even more tricky than offering a premium. Someone had to look after the horse during the nine months of the year when he was only a dangerous nuisance, eating his head off and doing nothing. Then, after three years or so, when his daughters were coming into use and a change of blood was required, selling him and buying a replacement bristled with occasions for argument and acrimony among the members scarcely less devastating than that which broke out if he suddenly died or became even temporarily incapacitated. Furthermore, it was difficult to get a good price when possible purchasers knew he had to be sold.

Societies for hiring a stallion by the season had been in existence in Scotland for about fifty years and the English had waited too long before imitating the practice, for it had all the advantages which Mr Bakewell had seen in it a hundred years before. The hirer, now a society rather than an individual, became a sort of partner with the owner. Each had an interest in the wellbeing of the horse and in seeing to it that the groom not only behaved himself but also, most importantly, played fair. James preferred, unless he could be assured of a local man's competence, to send his own groom and pay him, the fee taking this into account: if there was any question of fiddling, that brought the balance back in his own favour. The growth of the hiring club movement, following the pedigree society and the London Show, was the third development in the scheme for the improvement of cart horses. For the fourth and last we shall have to wait until 1920, when the Government used compulsory powers.

At this 1882 show, James had also entered a second horse in the senior class, the eight-year-old Tom of the Shires. Since he could not exhibit two horses simultaneously, he entrusted this one to Tom, who was now sixteen and far more competent than any of the paid men. When the final line-up was decided, Tom found himself standing above everyone else except his father. The horse was, in the judges' words, "a beautiful horse of the same type as Bar None, but a size smaller". Five weeks later, he was accompanying What's Wanted on the annual expedition to Lancashire. The single Forshaw stallion travelling here in 1815 was now regularly four. What's Wanted's card this year bore the words, 'He is now 9 years old. He is free from every spot or blemish, either natural or accidental, with legs and feet to wear out two sets of teeth, and action like a cob.' This was one he would never sell. A month later, on 22nd May, the horse collapsed and died.

In 1883, James won the four-year-old class with a new horse called St Ives. The following year, the number of horses exhibited in London was 359, of which 266 were stallions. The Angel's chief representative this time was a six-year-old black horse called King of Bucks. He won the full-aged class and was hired for the season by the Montgomery Entire Horse Association. This Welsh society, founded in 1876, had been the first, as an Irishman might say, to introduce the Scottish system into England. (It has operated without a break to this day and is now the oldest society in the world for promoting the breeding of any kind of horse.)

Now at last, an Extraordinary General Meeting at this 1884 London Show resolved that the English Cart Horse Society should be renamed the Shire Horse Society. This title had been advocated by some at the beginning but, since it seemed to exclude horses from the Fens or any area other than the English

Shires, there had been fierce opposition to it. It was accepted now simply because 'English Cart Horse' did not appear to indicate a breed at all. The Suffolk horse, after all, was English. As a brand name 'Shire' was to become, like 'Hoover', almost too successful. Some people today who have heard of other breeds of heavy horse imagine them to be Suffolk Shires, or Percheron or even Belgian Shires.

On Saturday morning 8th March, eight days after the London Show closed, Lawrence Drew dropped dead. He was 57. His Select Clydesdale Horse Society had 297 members in Scotland and six, including the Marquis of Londonderry at Seaham Harbour, County Durham, in England. The split which he had created in the Scottish ranks was not caused simply by his insistence that the Shire and the Clydesdale were really one breed. As the curious title of his Society hints, he also believed that a stud book was of no use unless the animals registered in it were themselves good individual specimens. In the preface to his Volume One (which at the time of his death was still waiting to go to the printer) he had written "While a horse may have a pedigree whose length is lost in the mist of the past, if it suffers from any hereditary disease which is at all likely to impair its usefulness ... it cannot gain admission here".

A colt could be registered in the Shire book as a yearling and its name would then appear in the volume published when it was barely two years old. Even a weed might have a pedigree. If well-grown and beautiful, a horse might be brought to the London Show. There, if possessing any inheritable defects, it would be rejected. but this did not prevent the owner from offering it to all and sundry, as long as they did not know – and of course the vast majority of pedigreed stallions did not set foot in London anyway. The problem, however, was wider and deeper than this. To meet the demands made upon him, the entire horse had to be lustful. But virility did not necessarily prove fertility. Nor was fertility the same as prepotency, the power to transmit to offspring more of his own characteristics than his partners contributed. In a system whereby in a single year one stallion might cover a hundred miscellaneous mares – patrician or plebian, big or small, handsome or ugly – a sound one, beautifully formed and prepotent as well, soon became a winner for his owner, for a legion of mare-owners and for the breed in general. Unfortunately, neither Drewism nor the show method could identify him. Forty years on, James's sons were to possess at the same time two London champions, one of which proved sterile and the other outstandingly fertile but utterly lacking in prepotency – and also two that never competed for the prize money but were prepotent in all the virtues of the breed.

Volume One of Mr Drew's stud book was duly published after his death, as were three subsequent ones. But the Select Clydesdale Horse Society was doomed to early collapse. His views about the identity of the Shire and Clydesdale breeds could not survive national prejudice and bigotry on both sides of the border.

6. A Visit in Jubilee Year

Rising nineteen, the very age at which his father had left home, Tom Forshaw had no desire to run away. Three inches or so shorter and built on a slightly smaller scale than James, he was a lieutenant, not a slave. On a Sunday, he did not have to scurry about in order to get across to the Priory Church where he had sung in the choir as a boy and was now showing every promise of developing a good baritone voice. For his part, James rejoiced that the omen of the twitching ear when the baby was in his mother's arms had proved reliable. Mary Ann's situation was now much changed from the rough old days at Burley. Few in the endless stream of visitors were paying customers at the inn. Horse customers took home to their wives glowing accounts of the charm and hospitality of Mrs Forshaw. And if she was an asset to James, Mary Ann junior, now seventeen, was a social and practical asset to both. Like mother, like daughter.

But what was to be done about the younger ones? Especially the three boys. James himself had been lucky to survive the lack of a good education. They must therefore have one and he now had the money to pay for it. There were two objections to a public school. Firstly, the snobbery would have been insupportable. The gentry treated him with respect when they spoke of cart horses, but it was too much to expect their sons to treat his as equals. Secondly, he was obsessed by the idea that young men who had to make their own way in the world should be able to speak foreign languages. No one ever learned these properly in England – and there were no business deals to be done in Latin or classical Greek. So he had put aside his fear of popery and packed Richard off to a Franciscan school he had learned about in Bruges. He was the naughty one, always in some sort of minor trouble, even in the church choir – and he loved singing. When he was about twelve, he had been sent home from practice one evening in disgrace, but was quite unabashed. He was the only boy who could get top G and they would have to have him back. His parents hoped that, now he was fifteen, the Franciscans would be able to teach him a bit of sense as well as languages. Agnes went to Bruges with him and Jim (11), and Billy (7) would follow. If Tom was conscious that this opportunity had not been available to him, in years to come, no one else ever noticed it. He could spell as accurately as anyone in the family.

Ten days before the late Mr Drew's horses were all sold up, Bar None went off with others to travel in the Fylde. In the middle of May, he suddenly went lame. So Tom was sent to Preston with a six-year-old substitute, a chestnut called Royal Sandy, and with instructions to hand him over to the groom and to get Bar None fit. He worked on the horse steadily for nearly a month and then wrote to tell his father that all was well but that there was so much work available that he proposed to take him on the road himself and leave the groom to continue with the substitute. At the end of the season, things had turned out very well.

Fig. 14 James Forshaw. This is the only known portrait.

The docile Royal Sandy, serving his mares with delicate nonchalance, was as popular as the robust Bar None, whose appetite for work was ravenous after his long layoff with a bad leg. And Tom became personally acquainted with "many real good Lancastrian farmers". The friendship he forged with their sons was to stand him in good stead, since the Fylde was always to be one of the most valued Forshaw connections.

The American market, boosted by the English pedigree system, was now at the height of its boom. James himself never went to the States, but now he thought that it was about time Tom did so. He therefore dispatched him in the autumn, in charge of a large consignment of stallions. In this he showed his customary guile. He was no less proud of Tom's appearance and manner of talking than he was of his abilities. All the leading Shire importers had heard of Mr Forshaw, for his name had become a byword in the States for reliability and fair dealing. If this nice young fellow was only the son, what must the father be like? James's reasoning was sound, as was his instruction that Tom should remain as long as there were influential people to be met.

The following February in London, Royal Sandy stood amiably at the head of the senior stallions' class. Mr Sanders Spencer, commenting on the Show, remarked "I hear that Royal Sandy was let for £500. If this be the case, then

Shire Horse breeding looks like proving to be one of the best means to lighten the agricultural depression". It was indeed the case, except that the Montgomery Association actually paid £575 for his services, as well as £275 for King of Bucks, who was paying them a second visit. However, more than the gilt was taken off this record-breaking gingerbread by a disaster. James had also brought St Ives to London, the first-prize four-year-old of two years before. He would not have done that if he had not considered he had an even better chance of the championship than Royal Sandy, for his general policy was not to show a horse again if it had won first prize. Arriving on the Monday in the unheated and badly ventilated Agricultural hall, St Ives quickly fell victim to the foul and stifling air of the day and the bitter foggy cold of the London February nights. He could not be brought into the ring on the Tuesday and died on the Friday.

In the fall of this year 1885, Tom was sent again to America, and for him the highlight of his trip was a visit to the Champaign Show, Illinois. Two cattle judges could not agree which of two Hereford bulls should be awarded the championship. Absurdly, there was no appointed referee. So the young gentleman from England was invited to step into the ring and pronounce upon the matter. The bull he favoured was called Caractacus, and his wisdom was so widely respected that Caractacus was never after that beaten in the show ring and became very famous throughout all the states of the Union – and in England too, where men were heard to say that it was wrong that so remarkably fine an animal should ever have been allowed to go abroad in the first place. This was silly talk. He was so fine only because a young horseman said he was – and in any case they themselves had never seen him.

A few weeks after the 1886 show, James read of the death of Burley-in-Wharfedale's most illustrious resident. In his later years W E Forster had not been very lucky. Mr Gladstone, forming his second Government in 1880, appointed him Chief Secretary for Ireland – perhaps wistfully thinking that anyone who could get the Education Bill through without splitting Church and State asunder and without widening the rift between Chapel and Church could cope with the Irish. He could not succeed but did survive the several attempts made on his life during the next two years and when in May 1882 his successor Lord Frederick Cavendish and Mr Burke the Under-Secretary were murdered in Phoenix Park he had even offered to go back to the job. Now, after a funeral service in Westminster Abbey his body was buried at Burley.

Any further recital of prizewinning stallions would make tedious reading. Let us therefore consult someone who actually saw them – all of them. It was a very refined and somewhat unctuous day visitor to the Angel at the end of March 1887 who represented that superior journal *Agriculture*. In fact, it was the editor himself, who thought it was high time to offer his readers inside information about the Forshaw enterprise. A fortnight later, he gave them two and a half pages of it, out of the sixteen in his paper.

"As a Shire Horse man," he wrote, "the genial Mr Forshaw stands at the top rung of the ladder, and it would be difficult indeed to say much of him that was not already known to all interested in the valuable work into which he throws his heart and soul, and in which he toils from early morn till late at night. In the prime of life, tall, of fine frame and physique and well proportioned, he looks, as the saying goes, 'as strong as a horse'. Accosting him, you are met by a pleasant face and pair of bright eyes, with a merry honest twinkle in them, and when he talks his voice and manner at once put you at your ease. There is in Mr Forshaw an immense amount of quaint, dry originality of humour, and the manner in which he relates his anecdotes is highly interesting to listen to."

Unfortunately, Mr Agriculture did not deem it prudent to print any of the stories, but he did mention that he had been met at Ranskill station by Tom, who drove him home behind a pony called Crafty. Crafty, the visitor thought, was enchanting. So was the exceedingly picturesque village of Blyth, "on the borders of the renowned old forest where the Merrie men were wont to roam". The fine old church "stood in a frame of tall wide-spreading patriarchal trees". Immediately opposite, on the old Roman road, was the Angel. This, he informed his readers, had a frontage of 120 feet, a possibly interesting fact. "Under its roof many a bowl of sack has been quaffed by celebrities of past times."

Margaret Forshaw (26), whose childhood had been spent in Lancashire, was now married to Charles Blackhurst, a vet in that county, and Richard was learning to become one. Agnes and Jim were away at their Belgian school. But the visitor did meet Mrs Forshaw, Miss Mary (now 20) and Master Bill (nearly 10). He did not venture to describe them – or, for that matter, Mr Tom – but he did go into raptures over the Lincoln sheep, a few Shorthorn heifers, a Hereford

Fig. 15 A month before Mr Agriculture's visit, Harold had become champion stallion at London – but James had long since sold him. The next fifty years were to prove him overwhelmingly the most influential sire of the breed.

bull, some Berkshire pigs, black-faced game fowls, a Collie dog and a fox terrier. His readers were no doubt whipped by this enthusiasm into a state of keen anticipation of what he might say of the horses. As was always the programme at Blyth, he did not see these until he had partaken of the excellent Forshaw hospitality, which invariably enhanced visitors' vision and ability to appreciate them. "Although Mr Forshaw's horses vary in size," he wrote "yet they are all of one type. To offer him anything without springy pasterns, wide feet, real flat bone and good quality hair is simply *an utter waste of time*. How often have we noticed in towns that horses possessing these most necessary points can do the most work – and that, while those with round bones, curly hair, steep pasterns and narrow feet cannot stand the paving-stones above two years at most, the flat bone, springy pastern and wide foot will wear quite five times as long a period?"

This rhetorical question so well expresses the essence of the Forshavian gospel that we may suspect that James himself had told Mr Agriculture what he had noticed so often as he walked to and from his London office.

If we include five yearlings and eleven two-year-olds, the visitor examined exactly forty stallions, which, although "all of one type", he severally described. In doing so he showed himself to be a master of synonyms, but the dish he set before his readers was a rich one, and today we do not have the stomach to do more than pick at some morsels of it.

His remarks about the yearlings were pretty feeble and were generally confined to noting that their sires were mostly Forshaw horses. For example, Carlton Chief, bred in the Fylde and a son of Ringleader, "looks like becoming a very big horse". Carlton Boss, by Blyth Echo, himself a son of What's Wanted, was "bred in the neighbourhood of Blyth by Henry Mellish Esq". We may be glad that the gushing editor chose to mention a member of this delightful family. The present Mr Mellish lived at Hodsock with his mother, whose late husband was a cousin of Colonel H F Mellish, the famous dandy who had gambled away the Blyth estate. He was a non-practising barrister, a member of the English Rifle VIII for very many years, a Fellow of the Royal Meteorological Society and Colonel of the 8th Battalion, Sherwood Foresters. Like his two sisters, who were adored locally for their generous works, he was unmarried. This Carlton Boss he had bred was "of great size for his age, but of high quality" (he had to be castrated the next year).

The visitor was a little puzzled by some of the two-year-olds, and it would seem that his pencil wavered until James explained that they were recent arrivals in poor condition. In a year's time proper feeding and care would make them like the three-year-olds – Carlton Hermit, for example, ("tremendously wide and thickset"), Prince Royal ("wonderful flat legs"), Carlton Blocky ("very blocky"), or Carlton Hero ("just the right kind for Nottinghamshire farmers").

The pencil became inspired by the four-year-olds. Carlton Farmer, "as he meets you, presents a wonderful breast, knee and foot." Carlton Hero had "deep shoulders, short back and wonderful hind quarters". Carlton Rattler possessed "a tremendous middle, wide chest and grand gait". Hydrometer "stands very near the ground and is a nearly perfect son of Premier". Blyth William was "very thick" and Carlton Comet "a brilliant black of the pure old wagon-horse breed. He has a very deep chest, with great arms and knees, and rare legs." Blyth Monarch ("handsome and square, with big legs and a lot of hair") was the only five-year-old. The two six-year-olds were Blyth Echo, "with tremendous shoulders and hind quarters" and Ringleader, who had "a great wide back". Royal Sandy, now eight, was as amiable as ever. "As we entered his box, this noble docile creature advanced to greet us and familiarly placed his face against ours." King of Bucks, a year older, was still on the staff. And so, of course, was Bar None himself, one year older again. As Mr Agriculture watched him being exercised, the party was joined by the celebrated Clydesdale breeder Peter Crawford of Strathblane, who said, "He is the best horse I ever saw. If he was a Clydesdale, his owner would have to refuse a very large sum to keep him. He's a horse down both sides". The genial owner grinned and said nothing. It would be a pity if he, rather than Mr Crawford, was quoted on this one. But, a hundred years later, we can still hear a Lancastrian rather than a Scottish or London voice behind the description of Young Blyth, now fifteen – the oldest horse on the place and the first that James had bought after moving to the Angel. "He looks no more than five years old. He has a wonderfully well-built top, the best quality of legs carrying nice silky hair, and good feet and pasterns. This old favourite is a very good getter. His stock wear like iron, and there are always plenty of farmers enquiring after him."

By the time the party saw the mares, all destined sooner or later to find permanent owners, descriptive powers were waning and were confined to brief remarks such as "very wide and heavy-set" and "very thick and cloggy". Nevertheless, determined to see all, Mr Agriculture inspected two hackney mares and re-inspected the entrancing Crafty. Before she took him back to the station, he sat over the teacups, examined oil paintings of What's Wanted, Bar None and others, looked at all the silver cups and was told that Mr Forshaw ground all his own corn, always used moss litter because it was better for feet than straw, contracted annually for shoeing, employed twelve men all the year round and, of course, many more in the spring and summer – but if he tried to discover any secrets, for example about feeding, he prised none from the jovial Mr Forshaw. The only thing he learned which he could not have seen for himself was that the litter was always bought from J P Taylor's Moss Litter Company of Newcastle-on-Tyne. Even when he mentioned Mr Forshaw's great reputation for integrity, all he got in reply was that it was "no uncommon thing for an electric flash to arrive at Blyth from the Continent of America ordering Shires which the buyer has never seen but is perfectly content that the seller should select for him".

Except for Shire breeding, the farming scene was one of unmixed gloom. *Agriculture* on 13th April which contained the editor's uncritical critique of the Blyth stallions, carried a resumé of a fighting speech about the depression delivered by S W Poynter of Great Wakering in Essex to a thousand members of several Farmers' Clubs crammed into the Assembly Room of the Grand Hotel in Bristol. The meeting unanimously called for the abandonment of free imports and the formation of a National Association of Farmers. *Agriculture* applauded this. The farming interest, through lack of unity and combination, was thoroughly neglected and thereby "to a deplorable extent ruined". In the correspondence columns, J E Jarvis furiously attacked someone who had suggested that half the hops in Kent should be grubbed up. "One of the most recent remedies of the hard times I have heard of is that we must plant the land with asparagus. It is enough to make us feel sick, and almost savage."

As in all old newspapers, it is the inconsequential items that are often the most revealing of their period. This issue of *Agriculture* reported that the tenants of Lord Windsor had had a 10% remittal of their rents, which on this Worcestershire estate had now been reduced by 30% since 1878. Mr Edmund Beck, agent to the Sandringham estate (and, like all Becks, an enthusiastic supporter of the Shire horse) had been severely injured when thrown from his horse. In the advertisement columns the Rev Joseph Holmes of Bloomsbury Square announced that "after suffering a number of years from Nervous Debility and Physical Exhaustion (from the errors and indiscretions of youth) and trying in vain every known remedy, he has at last, during his travels in Old Mexico, found a remedy which entirely cured and saved him from death". To anyone who sent him a stamped addressed envelope, he would divulge the secret free of charge. For simple intestinal upsets, however, one still had to pay. Beecham's Pills cost 1s 11/2d or 2s 9d, though of course they were, as always, worth a guinea a box, especially if the bowels were sufficiently disordered to cause Frightful Dreams. Arthur Perkins of Hanley, aged two and a half, had been eating biscuits when he was attacked by a gamecock, and was now dead. So life continued, faltered or stopped.

By the time this issue of *Agriculture* was being digested, Royal Sandy, Ringleader and Blyth Echo, Hydrometer, Royal William and Carlton Thumper had all left for Preston, where they were paraded in a pub yard of the Castle Hotel before taking up their various routes (Thumper was only two, and his task was to assist where necessary, and learn his job). Most of the other Blyth horses were also already on their rounds, distant or near. Old Young Blyth was standing at home. Bar None had gone to Carlton-on-Trent, where Tom was due to go and live in preparation for a big Forshaw migration.

Back at Blyth, the Queen's Golden Jubilee was celebrated on 21st June with a church service, followed by children's sports in the grounds of the Hall. Even Mrs Walker came up trumps, for she sparingly provided tea. The big parish tea, on the other hand, was produced by 29 ladies of the village, including Mrs Forshaw. After that there were adult sports in Mr Forshaw's field, prize giving on the Green at 9 o'clock and, finally, dancing to the music of an accordian until midnight.

Next year, Blyth celebrated the octo-centenary of the endowment of the Benedictine Priory. But the Forshaw family was by now in new pastures.

7. Up the Line to Carlton

For some years, James had been looking out for new premises. The Angel and the Mill Farm had several drawbacks. One was that he did not own them and Mrs Walker, who did, could not be persuaded to carry out any but minimal repairs. The deepening agricultural depression was closing her miserly fist tighter still. In any case, his business had grown so large and so specialist that even the most expensive adaptations would not have sufficed. In addition, the land had a sandy bottom and the grass dried up in summer, when it was most needed.

Another disadvantage was the railway. Horses had to be walked to Ranskill station and were sometimes loaded in a heated condition. Illness occasionally followed, and death once. James himself was endlessly travelling, and the slow stopper delayed the start of his journeys and held up his return at night, unless he was driven the seven miles to or from Retford. There was only one daily delivery of mail at Blyth, and that not until ten o'clock. Often he began a long journey before a letter cancelling or altering the appointment arrived. In short, the place which provided a heaven-sent opportunity in 1874 was, only a dozen years later, inadequate and unsatisfactory.

It was the Ranskill station master who found the ideal new place. In 1884 he was transferred up the main Great Northern line to Carlton-on-Trent and had not been there many months before he learned of a farm of about 100 acres which would be shortly coming up for sale – near the station and adjoining the line. He wrote to James, who came to have a look. From Ranskill, it was an easy seventeen mile journey by the Great Northern main line stopper, calling at Barnby Moor, Retford (change for the Sheffield – Grimsby line), Tuxford, Dukeries Junction (change for Chesterfield-Lincoln), Crow Park and Carlton-on-trent. The next station after Carlton was Newark (North Gate) and from there or from the Midland Railway's Castle station you could go almost anywhere.

He went over the ground with his friend and learned that, considering he was doing so much business with the Great Northern, he would probably be able to have express trains stopped by request – and sixty or seventy went through the station every 24 hours. He was excited. The land was clayey, beneficial to horses' feet and excellent for their stomachs, for it would give good grass. The existing farm house would be suitable for the head man. All the other buildings would be new. He walked to a certain spot in the middle of a field and said, "This is where my office will be." Then he drove his walking stick into the ground, adding "And here I shall have my chair, so that I can watch the horses." He went home pleased. He came back with Mary Ann, and she was pleased. So he bought the property.

Over the next two years, he planned and replanned the position of every building and the arrangement of all the paddocks. He set about improving the grass. He negotiated with the GNR which provided him with a loop line on which he built a private loading dock. In return for the wayleave granted to the company to lay the track on his land, he received the right in perpetuity to ask for any express train to be halted at the station for the convenience of the family or visitors. Horse boxes, coupled to the rear of passenger trains, could be hauled by a shunting horse to or from the dock.

He designed the stud buildings himself, and the first to be completed comprised two rows each of thirteen boxes facing inwards and, between them, a lofty corridor 180 feet long and 24 feet wide, roofed with glass. The doors to the boxes, numbered in black paint eight inches high, were of two-inch timber reinforced to a height of three feet by kick-proof cross-battens six inches thick. They had large iron latches and fifteen-inch sliding bolts which could be padlocked if necessary. Each box had its own yard so that its inhabitant could choose for himself whether to be indoors or out. The corridor could be used as a parade for showing horses or exercising them in bad weather. The same block also included the cookhouse, steam engine room, office, overhead granaries, harness room with a fireplace for the grooms and sliding-door cupboards to store horse blankets, and also the dispensary.

This was followed by another group of 30 boxes, without separate yards, 11 boxes exposed to the fresh air, two stables each with six stalls, two boxes at a distance from all others for use as an isolation hospital, a farrier's shop, staff accommodation and a gas works to provide all lighting, including that of the railway siding, and everything else that he believed would make a model establishment. The rest of the land was divided into twenty paddocks of differing sizes by post-and-rail fencing, and hawthorn was planted along the lines as a hedge (as with everything else, the fence was of such a quality that, when dismantled sixty years later, it was perfectly serviceable for use elsewhere). Wells, four feet in diameter, were sunk to a depth of sixty feet in the paddocks to save carting water.

When the editor of *Agriculture* visited Blyth in the spring of 1887, work was just beginning on the Forshaw house at Carlton – three sitting-rooms, nine bedrooms, two kitchens and an office. James reckoned that on several occasions he had nearly died from inflammation of the lungs through sleeping in damp beds. So hot water pipes ran through the walls of the upper floor, and Mary Ann intended to keep to her usual plan of distributing the family round the various rooms in turn when there were no visitors. Her rule was that no bed should be unoccupied for more than three consecutive nights.

All the bricks were being hauled from the station yard by a nine-year-old stallion, Better Times. This ignominious occupation kept him fit, and he would be ready to serve a cheap sort of mare or two when the season began (James had once possessed two Better Times, of exactly the same age, but the other was now in Illinois). When the season did begin, Tom went to live in the little farmhouse with his sister Mary to superintend the domestic arrangements while he supervised the final building work.

He brought with him Bar None, who served at £4 a time and 5/- the groom. Five shillings! That showed the customers the class of establishment they were

Fig. 16 The main building at Carlton-on-Trent.

dealing with. The paddocks began to fill with mares lodging at 7/- a week, or 8/6 for a mare and foal. The horse was busier than he had ever been, partly because it was so easy to send mares to the new place and partly because of his increasing reputation as something more than just another London champion. His progeny were becoming known for the quality of their legs and feet and for an unfailing share of his own great bone, powerful hindquarters and deep shoulders. His companion, Better Times, fortunately for his pride, did not have to pull the mares in their boxes from the station into the siding before serving them or allowing his more famous colleague to do so. This work had to be done by a gelding on the GNR shunting staff.

On the wall of the parade building facing the main line was already painted the legend FORSHAW'S SHIRE HORSES in black letters six feet high against a white background, to catch every idle eye that looked from the windows of trains. If the ghost of good old Dan Howsin, whose stallions had lived within a mile or two of here, ever roamed the fields, he would have been astonished to see this modern establishment, the first and only commercial Shire stallion headquarters to be purpose-built. He might have ignored the changes in the roads, just as phantoms in houses where floors have been raised or lowered prefer to walk on the old level or pass through blocked doorways. That which now gave access only to the farm was part of the old road from Norwell to Sutton-on-Trent and local people would for some years still call it Dead Man's Dyke. James was renaming it Stud Lane, which was less creepy for anyone who might fear to see a corpse in the ditch.

In designing his stud farm, he stared as far into the future as he could. He told Tom that, one day, horsepower would be superseded and no one would want Shire stallions any more. So he showed how the main building was so positioned that the siding could be extended straight down the parade. "If you or your sons have to sell this place one day as a factory," he said, "that is where people will be able to load up the trucks." Tom was impressed by his long-sightedness, but dismissed the possibility as a sort of nightmare.

The family moved to Carlton in the spring of 1888, and a fortnight later James found that a nightmare which had haunted him for months was in fact the living truth. He had never taken a holiday. Every year he had worked harder than the year before. On all his increasing travels, he had neglected meals. He wrote all his own correspondence and kept his own books. He regularly sat up half the night to clear the letters and papers on his desk before setting off on the first train of the morning to look at horses or buy them. For some months he had pretended to himself that he was not ill, but one morning he was simply incapable of rising from his bed. Mary Ann had begged him in vain to take medical advice. Now she sent for a doctor, who called in a consultant.

He was taken to Harrogate. Mary Ann was constantly at his bedside and the specialist visited him five times a day. When, after a month, it was clear that he was going to survive, she left to tackle the unresolved problems of organising a new house. Mary junior took her place at Harrogate and patiently bore the complaints and irritability of a convalescent who kept demanding to be allowed home and took no pleasure in little walks on warm days or being wrapped in a warm rug on cold ones. What catastrophes at home, he kept asking, were being concealed from him?

On his eventual return, he was filled by a mixture of disappointment and pride when he found nothing to criticise. During that autumn and winter, he was far too weak to do anything except sit in his study chair and gaze at the stallions being walked. It was essential that a horse should be exercised not only adequately but correctly, even on the worst of winter days – smartly going and head up as if the eyes of a show judge were constantly upon him. What groom could be trusted to do that, unless he knew that the boss might be watching – from start to finish of every mile out and all the way back, even with the last stallion in the afternoon, when his arm was weary of being held so high?

If a man flagged and fell below perfection, James could let off his pent-up emotion by shouting at Tom. Richard had interrupted his veterinary training to be a useful assistant to his elder brother. So James could shout and swear at him, too. Mary Ann, who was a loving mother as well as a good wife, had occasion sometimes to remind him that no one would want him to get like his father. The mere suggestion of such a comparison was an outrage but, if used sparingly, a salutary one.

When Tom took Hydrometer into the London ring the following February and won the class for senior "short-legged" stallions (under 16.2 hands), James was a proud father. This horse, now six, had had a show career that was now becoming typical for a Forshaw stallion. It was his third successive appearance in London, where he had stood fourth in his class, then second, and now top. The championship would have been beyond his short reach, for this inevitably went to the best of the taller horses. So it would be pointless to show him again. He could either use his position to command a higher fee from now on, or go for sale to a gentleman with the money to buy winners. He was in fact bought by the Duke of Marlborough and went to Blenheim.

The beginning of the Nineties saw the sudden collapse of the American market. James had foreseen trouble and had stopped sending horses there except on a guaranteed sale. "Many other exporters," he later said, "went on buying in a reckless manner, and I warned them. But they found their stables full of horses of no quality or marketable value in England and their pockets full of "I owe yous" for horses already taken. It was many a year before they recovered themselves, and many never did so." He managed to increase his trade with Russia, Germany and Australia. One Australian visitor was so enamoured of the Carlton scene that he presented him with a nugget of pure gold. The best customer by far, however, was now Argentina, where the buyers wanted a better animal than the United States had ever desired, and paid a better price.

He had always been a staunch Church of England man and, as soon as he had recovered his health, began to attend Carlton church where Tom was singing in the choir. Colonel Craig, a little man of great importance who wore built-up boots to make it easier for others to recognise his status, took exception to this cart-horse feller sitting so far up the church. He instructed the vicar, Richard Robinson, to tell him to sit farther back. The intrepid parson stoutly refused, saying that at Carlton all seats were free. A little later, salt was rubbed into the Colonel's punctured pride when he demanded that a London express be stopped for him. When he was told that this was impossible, he retorted, "You do it for that horse-dealer." The station-master saw his opportunity to lower him by a peg or two, and invited him into his office. He told his clerk to turn up Colonel Craig's account. There was no account. "Find Mr James Forshaw's account." It was very large. The Colonel grunted and walked out. When he later discovered that the Forshaw feller was sufficiently acceptable to the Prince of Wales as to have received an invitation to shoot at Sandringham, he began to change his tune and played the first notes on leaving church with a "Come over for a glass of sherry before luncheon." – but the tune was never completed or the harmony added, because James always found an excuse. "I've no time to drink sherry with that sort of bugger," he told Tom.

The move to Carlton had deprived farmers in the Blyth area of the use of those of his stallions that happened to be standing at home during the season, and some of them now came to ask his advice about what to do. He urged them to form a hiring society on the new model, for this would give them the freedom to choose a horse from any stallion owner in the country. So they set up the Worksop, Blyth and District Shire Horse Association, but the members did not want to look anywhere else than Carlton and hired from him. He also recommended them to become corporate members of the Shire Horse Society and in February 1891 they were duly elected – only the fourth in the country to take this sensible step after the South Devon Horse Association, the Chester Farmers' Club and the Winslow Stud Shire Horse Society in Buckinghamshire. (The Worksop Association was to collapse in 1906 after a row. After that, a stallion was regularly sent from Carlton on a private enterprise route, and everyone seemed happy with that.)

James had always been so busy that he had consistently refused to stand for the Council of the breed society but now, with Tom taking more and more responsibility at home, he allowed his name to go forward and was elected in February 1892. He now seemed fully fit again and always arrived at the stables very early in the morning. The men took care to note the manner of his coming. If he was whistling, that was a bad sign, though on the whole a rare one.

Towards the end of the season this year, Bar None began to show signs of his age. He was now fifteen and died of heart disease on 6th October. James knew to a guinea how much money he had earned in fees. The loss of the Forshaw records means that we do not, but it must have totalled about £4,500 He wondered what profit he had brought to others. So he sat down with Tom one evening and they began adding up how many live foals he had procreated. The total was just over a thousand. Then they listed the prices that the better-known of them had been sold for, and were astounded. His place at the head of the stud had already been taken by Honest Tom 5123 (to identify this horse, it is necessary to quote his stud book number, because 75 Honest Toms had already been registered). This massive creature had been bred by Thomas Mott at Littleport, near Ely. Now, at the age of eight, he weighed 26 cwt (1.3 tons) and stood 17.1 hands high (5ft 9 ins) at the shoulder.

Meanwhile, one fine summer's day Tom had been sitting on a gate near Norwell, a mile or so from home, when a girl rode past. He raised his hat. She smote him in the heart with a smile and rode on, leaving him in a trance. Partially recovered, he floated home to tell his sister Mary that, when he had found out who she was, he was going to marry this girl.

She was, he discovered, Bessie or, more formally, Sarah Elizabeth Swift. To understand the circumstances of her appearance on horseback before Tom's impressionable eyes, it is necessary to go back a little way into history. Her father Thomas Swift had been one of a family which had farmed for generations at Kirton Skelsdyke a mile or so from where the Welland flows into the Wash. In some, now inexplicable, way he had met and married a farmer's daughter from Cumberland, but his father's opposition to the match was so vigorous that he decided to take his bride to Australia to look for gold. They had two children there – Thomas junior and Bessie who was born on 25th October 1864. The couple never found any gold and died in Australia. So the son and daughter came back to England. Young Thomas took a holding at Norwell and Bessie went north to live with Uncle Charles Swift, until he proved so difficult and strict that she left him and took up nursing at Birkenhead. After only two years of this she learned that her brother needed help on his farm and so she came to join him. This was the most romantic story Tom had ever heard. Luckily for him the path from infatuation to true mutual love ran smooth and when he and Bessie were married on 14th November 1893 they moved to Scotfield, a new house on the stud farm built specially for them. She was 29 and he eight months younger.

His brother Richard had now joined a veterinary practice at Spalding and was playing a lot of cricket – at which he excelled in spite of a total lack of coaching from the Franciscan brothers in Belgium. James strongly disapproved. Cricket took far too much time and was quite unsuitable for a young man at the start of his career. However, after listening to two strangers in a train talking

Fig. 17 At the 1893 London Show Forshaw's Orchard Prince, senior cup winner, is on the left. Lord Belper's yearling, chosen as champion, has knocked his groom flat and is running away. The Prince of Wales is not alarmed. (Depicted in *The Illustrated Sporting and Dramatic News*.)

about the prospects for a match at Lincoln the following Saturday and expressing their opinion that the key factor would be Forshaw's bowling, he changed his mind and began to boast about him.

James was always talking to men in trains and on one journey the conversation turned to the great American depression. This reminded him how lucky he had been over this, but he did have in his wallet a bill amounting to £400, two years overdue. "I pulled it out and showed it to them," he later wrote "and said, to show them what faith I had in it, that any of them could have it for five shillings. None of them seemed anxious to accept, so I put it back. When I got home and was looking through my letters, there was one enclosing a cheque for two hundred pounds from this very man, and a promise to send the remaining money very soon. After a short time it came. He also came later in person and began to buy once more. He turned out to be a real good man and we did lots of business together for years after that."

The third son Jim had now left school and joined the business, working mainly at the books and correspondence, though he was also learning the farm side and was expected to become a better horseman than a non-Forshaw. Father celebrated the family progress by buying another 120 acres at home and also the 70-acre Ruddingwood Farm at Tuxford, five miles away, where he fed cattle and ran a number of mares and fillies.

As the Nineties progressed, the care that had gone into the planning of the premises proved its value. On one occasion, twenty-four stallions were loaded into boxes at the siding in twenty-five minutes, using all available hands. About £1,900 a year was spent on the purchase of cake and corn. Otherwise the land produced enough feed for the seventy horses that were generally on the place, though coming and going made the numbers fluctuate constantly. From August to the middle of December, stallions were turned out day and night into the paddocks – one or three or more in each, but never two. Two would fight, but a greater number would soon sort out their ranking. "This freedom cools down their legs and feet, and altogether renews them," James used to say. "The consequence is, their progeny is full of vitality." They were handfed when running at grass, and the appetite and individual requirement of each horse was studied with great care.

In 1896 seven stallions were hired out to various societies and seventeen travelled privately on routes that ranged from Thisk to Swindon. The following year, the total travelling was 28, and this side of the enterprise now began to form a steadily increasing proportion of the business. Two senior stallions served mares at Carlton, together with a further fifteen which were also available as substitutes to relieve any of those that were away. An early telegram in the morning would enable a horse to be boxed and dispatched to reach any destination in England before nightfall. No one else could provide such a service.

FORSHAW'S SHIRE HORSES.

HONEST TOM 5,123
AND
DOUBLE TOM 14,595.

Will Stand at the STUD FARM, CARLTON-ON-TRENT, near Newark.

RAILWAY—G.N. MAIN LINE.

Terms (by Nomination)—**5 Guineas** each, and Grass Keeping for Single Mares at 6s. per week, and Mare and Foal 8s. 6d. per week. Corn given according to instructions at market prices. Grass ready about April 25th.

HONEST TOM 5,123.

HONEST TOM 5,123 is well known as a getter of the Best and Soundest Stock in the kingdom. Note his record at the leading Shows for the past three years, also the number of horses got by him kept entire in these days when *weight* and *substance*, with SOUNDNESS, are required.

Note the result of London Show, 1894, where Nine Animals are entered got by him, and every one PASSED the VETS., with result as follows : FIVE Prizes, one H.C., and one C. ; and some immense prices realised.

DOUBLE TOM 14,595, Bay, is a member of that marvellous family of Honest Tom's 5,123, and the dam of Double Tom is a brown mare of enormous weight and character, and sound. Pedigree : Sire, Honest Tom 5,123 (Forshaw's) ; dam, Bright by Honest Tom 3,144 ; granddam, Flower by Rutland Hero 1,908. Limited to 20 mares at £5 5s. each.

For Pedigrees see Stud Books. Cards and Particulars will be forwarded on application to the Owner,

JAMES FORSHAW, Carlton-on-Trent, near Newark.

P.S.—Station Five Minutes' Walk from this Stud. All parties interested in Shire Horses are welcome to View this Stud.

Fig. 18 A typical advertisement in *The Live Stock Journal*. Double Tom, a son of Honest Tom, was spotted on his veterinary rounds by Richard, who bought him and then sold him on to his father.

Sometimes other stallion-owners, desperate after one or two horses had gone wrong, sent an urgent plea for help, which was attended to as promptly and thoughtfully as if it had been a message from a Carlton groom. It was all good for future business. More spectacular profits were made of course from sales, especially of horses which a keen eye had originally selected as two-year-olds or yearlings in poor condition. One such horse was sold for £2,000, and four together for just over £6,000, though these figures were exceptional. At this time, James was also breeding on a fairly extensive scale, for not all the mares he handled were intended for sale until they had been proved for fertility and their foals were also available to be sold.

Whenever he was asked, and that was frequently, to account for his success, his answer was not particularly illuminating. Nor is that surprising, for the question is always a silly one; he used to please the press by giving them three reasons that they could write about – and then realise that they had been fobbed off with platitudes. Firstly, he used to say, "I try to have every horse a little larger than the horses of other people." Secondly, he paid particular attention to soundness. And thirdly, he studied those strains of blood which wore best. "Some stallions," he would say, "get produce which is full of bloom and full of promise when they are extremely young, but come to nothing at maturity. This is the sort I steer clear of." Not he, but people who knew him would have added that he had more brains than others and used them for more hours in a day. And they would have mentioned his absolute integrity in a way of business that was noted for sharp practice.

There was now in 1897, and had been for some years, only one professional stallion-owner in England who could be compared with him. This was John Adcock Barrs of Nailstone in Leicestershire, who had now won 72 London prizes with 58 different animals. James had won 82 prizes, with 63. Eleven of James's awards were firsts with nine different horses – and the supreme championship with Bar None. John had had five firsts, with four horses, and had collected ten awards at this last show against James's nine. But less than four months after the show he died at the age of 47. Seventeen of his stallions were busy on their rounds in various parts of the country. Unlike James, who used 'Carlton' only occasionally, all his stallions were named with the Nailstone prefix, unless of course they had been already registered when he bought them. As his memorial in pedigree history, there are 242 'Nailstones' foaled between 1881 and 1896 in the stud book, 23 of them bred by himself. Their names range from the orthodox to the eccentric, such as Nailstone Ascetic, Bludgeon and Bruiser, Clencher, Demon, Extinguisher, Fanatic, Go Bang, Hermit and so on through Jack-of-all-Trades and Rod-in-Pickle to Wideawake. There are also 87 'Nailstone' mares that had passed through his hands or were bred by him.

There was a sale and James bought a two-year-old, Nailstone Coeur-de-Lion, which had been highly commended in a class of 66 at London. Several bidders saw something extra good in him and he had to pay 710 guineas, but it was a good buy, for he was just the sort that he always went for. John's widow Annie determined to carry on the business on a smaller scale, with the help of

John Warner Adcock Barrs, the only one of her four sons to have survived childhood. He was only fifteen but showed every promise of being as good a man as his father.

At the London Show of 1900, James was one of the judges. This was never a congenial duty, as it prevented him from showing his own horses. In addition, he already knew the merits of so many of the older exhibits (that is, their breeding worth, which was the most important thing about them) that it was not easy to forget what he knew and concentrate only on their excellence as individual specimens at the particular moment they stood before him. However, he did his duty, and looked forward to the next year.

He was approaching his sixtieth birthday, and the furious activity of his life was taking its toll. One day, finding his hand shaky, he threw all his cigars into the fire. At the end of the year, he made Tom and Jim his partners and the firm became J Forshaw & Sons.

8. J Forshaw & Sons

James's large advertisements in the farming press, invariably headed by evangelistic mottoes, always concentrated on the two stallions standing at Carlton in the coming season and instead of a list of their prizes, as other owners liked to include, there was a mini-sermon. In 1901 Jim, on behalf of the new partnership, produced the banner headline 'BREED THE BEST IF YOU BREED AT ALL'. Nailstone Coeur-de-Lion, the colt purchased at the late John Barrs' dispersal sale, winner of a first prize at London when four and now six, was described as the "best stock horse of the Shire breed at the present day". And why? Because he was "bred up to it, as a careful perusal of his pedigree will explain to all who know the best and soundest strains of blood". His colleague at home was King Holt, an eight-year-old whose "power of putting his progeny upon the proper kind of feet and pasterns thoroughly entitles him to be called a specialist. The results from mares with only very moderate feet and joints are marvellous." The fee for either stallion was seven guineas.

There was a two-line title in 1902:
'SIZE SUBSTANCE SOUNDNESS
NOTICE: UNSOUND STALLIONS ARE WORTHLESS'
Nailstone Coeur-de-Lion was again at home and was partnered by the ten-year-old Stroxton Tom. A warning was included that maiden fillies must not be sent to either of these exceptionally lusty heavyweights.

Before the series of advertisements this year had run its course, Stroxton Tom won the supreme championship at London – the oldest horse by two years ever to have done so, as this beauty contest tended to favour the young and sprightly. His story is a good example of James's acumen. Diamond, his dam, was owned by Charles Lynn of Church Farm, Stroxton (pronounced 'Strawson'), near Grantham, who regularly used Forshaw stallions on her. In 1892, when she was eight, she had a colt foal by Honest Tom 5123 and was taken to the Grantham Show, where she won first prize. In the foals class, her little son stood bottom. James was there. Whereas the judge had to look at a poor foal, he saw a future horse. He offered £50 for him. Lynn's groom, Charlie Burrell, was canny and persuaded his boss not to sell.

Three years later, the colt had been neither sold nor castrated nor put in the stud book. The Forshaws had another shot at acquiring him. Some meddler, possibly with his own eye on him, started a rumour that his wind was broken. Charles Lynn, enraged, called in a vet, who pronounced the animal sound. So James got him at last – for over £300. Mr Lynn then had to rush around getting a lot of pedigree papers signed and countersigned, for he had never registered a single one of his horses, though they were all purebred. In the 1896 volume, eight Shires bred by him all appeared at once, including Stroxton Tom and his dam, now called Stroxton Diamond.

James took his purchase to London, where he was highly commended, and then waited five years. In 1901, exhibited by 'J Forshaw & Sons', he appeared a second time and won the class for big stallions. He also took the senior cup for the best stallion over three. When the judges preferred the junior cup winner, a two-year-old, for the supreme championship, they provoked an uproar in the Royal Agricultural Hall such as had never been heard before, and achieved for themselves instant unpopularity.

The following year, he won the senior cup again. The junior champion was Lord Rothschild's Birdsall Menestrel, bred by Lord Middleton. This was a near-perfect young animal but the judges did not repeat their predecessors' mistake. They chose the ten-year-old as champion of 476 stallions packed into the stifling Agricultural Hall for those four February days and nights.

The King came into the ring to present the gold cup to old James. The applause was deafening. Stroxton Tom, excited, spun round suddenly and knocked his surprised owner with his hock. The lid of the cup flew into the air and landed ten yards away. The horse plunged off in the same direction and James hurried to retrieve him. When they returned to their place, the King had disappeared from the ring. His portly Majesty, as knowledgeable as any man about the temperament and weight of Shire stallions, skimmed to safety across the tan like a duck flapping over water.

A craze was now beginning to sweep through the land for an abundance of long hair on Shire legs, fostered by the notion that this was a necessary indication of good strong bone beneath. Tom Fullard, member of a family with a long history in breeding Fens horses, symbolised the new idea. He named one of his

Fig. 19 *The Graphic*'s artist depicts the response of stallions to clapping and cheering in the Royal Agricultural Hall.

stallions There's 'Air. James was very critical of this theory. "The hair doesn't pull anything", he used to say. "Nor does the head". In addition he had known only too well from his Manchester and Bradford days that the "feather" of Shires, intrinsic and attractive to the eye, made it difficult to clean the legs properly. The more of it there was, the more likely was its wearer to develop 'grease'. In its early stages this waxy discharge caused irritation and made the horse stamp or rub a hind leg against the other. As it progressed it became incurable. The hairs were gummed together, the skin thickened and warty growths developed. When fully grown, these were usually called 'grapes' though their only similarity to bunches of that fruit was visual, for their stink was appalling.

The two junior partners agreed with their father in principle, but would have to run the business after he had gone. They suggested he should make at least some obeisance to hair. "If we don't," they said, "we'll be left behind." James did not take kindly to the idea of being left behind, and Tom managed to turn the new fashion to the firm's advantage, for, like the old man, he was a master of every detail that would enhance a horse's appearance. As a good coiffeur can improve the shape of a human head, so can the gifted equine hairdresser improve the pastern. "Give me some hair," he used to say, "and I can make a leg."

In 1903, James's health was beginning to fail and he handed the London Show responsibilities entirely to Tom. In judging the fifty four-year-olds, Messrs William Richardson from Cambridgeshire and Joseph Grimes (Derbyshire) "unhesitatingly plumped for substance", as the Farmer and Stockbreeder expressed it in explaining why the Forshaws' Lord Mayor II was top. It was Grimes and another Derbyshire man, John Nix, who judged the 27 short-legged contenders and they followed the example of their predecessors in the two preceding years by choosing Capstone Harold, also from Carlton, "the evergreen sire of perennial freshness, a remarkably thick well-proportioned horse. To use a nautical term, his displacement would be considerable." Among the 44 big stallions, Nix and Richardson could not decide between Fledboro' Minor (also seven, but making his first appearance for the firm in town) and Mr Peter Stubs' Blaisdon Conqueror from the Forest of Dean. Mr Grimes came in as referee and was subjected to noisy advice from rival Gloucestershire and Nottingham supporters. He preferred the Forshaw horse. Stroxton Tom (whose service fee was now ten guineas) easily won the veterans class again, and then beat his three Carlton colleagues for the senior cup.

The contest for the supreme championship was a repeat of the previous year's cup final. Lord Rothschild's Menestrel had filled out wonderfully as a three-year-old, whereas ripe old Tom, surely, could now be only a little overripe. All three judged entered the ring together and meticulously refreshed their memories by running their hands down every leg and peering attentively at every part of the equine anatomy. Time and time again the two horses were sent to walk and trot round the ring, each drawing salvos of applause from its supporters. There were repeated warnings from the stewards and other officials that anyone who upset the horses would be ejected – but it was impossible to throw everybody out of the Hall, and the shouting and clapping continued, making an amazing din. The Edwardians would be astonished to find the judging at modern shows conducted in solemn silence and the result greeted by mild applause.

Messrs Richardson and Grimes at last made their minds up – differently. John Nix just could not decide. At last, as Birdsall Menestrel showed his paces for the umpteenth time, he shook his head. It was all over, and Stroxton Tom at the age of eleven became the oldest horse ever to win the championship, before or since his time. "Like good wine," said the Farmer and Stockbreeder, "he improves with age. With substance to satisfy the greatest stickler for that commodity, he sacrifices nothing in freshness of limb, joints and feet." He was a hundredweight heavier than in 1902, but "hundredweights count for little when the ton has been left far behind".

However, the excitement was not finished. The championship cup was presented by the Prince of Wales, standing in for his father who, when he heard the name of the winner this time, was no doubt glad that he had been unable to attend. It was received by Tom, deputising for his father. The Princess bravely accompanied her husband into the ring. This set the applause going with gusto and it reached a crescendo as the cup was being handed over. Stroxton Tom set off again. Tom was unable to pull him round because that would have knocked their Royal Highnesses for six. But the horse swerved of his own accord, Tom shouted "heighup", the Princess grabbed the Prince's arm, Stroxton Tom brushed past them and then cleared a chair and knocked an attendant flying. If the future George V had been squashed utterly flat, it would have been a tragedy, because he later became an even greater expert in Shire-breeding than his father and one of the most enthusiastic supporters of the London Show that there ever was.

Incidentally, if Lord Rothschild's young horse had beaten Stroxton Tom in that final judgement, he would have scored a remarkable double, for his Solace won the mares championship. And it was therefore a pity that the King was absent, for he was her breeder. His £10 prize for that had to be posted to him.

When all the class winners, male and female, paraded amid relative calm, Tom led Stroxton Tom and Richard, Jim and William Forshaw the other three. "Which is the prouder," someone was heard to say in the stand, "Mrs Forshaw of her sons, or Mr Forshaw of his horses?"

Commenting on the Show in general, the Farmer and Stockbreeder remarked that "it is the eighth wonder of the world that in the confined space at the Hall more people are not injured." The reporter forbore to mention other dangers, but Tom Forshaw, in an article many years later, wrote that in those times "men regarded the London Show as an excuse for enjoyment and occasionally, I am afraid, for carousal. Grooms were not always in that clear-headed condition essential to the proper showing of horses. This often led to indifference and sometimes to careless and even dangerous handling. Unless the master was prepared to give personal attention, his horses, like his men, did not always go into the ring at their best. People were kicked, and minor accidents were frequent." He had inherited his father's gift for understatement. This year, however, only the airborne attendant and one spectator were injured and they gamely struggled to their feet again.

On returning home, Jim wrote to Charles Lynn. "Dear Sir, Allow us to congratulate you on breeding the best Shire that ever won the Cup in London and the best sire that walks. A colt by him topped the sale after the show. We shall be delighted to show you the old boy whenever you can find the time to come. With kind regards, J Forshaw and Sons." Mr Lynn treasured this letter and it is still preserved today, but he knew how big a part is played by luck in horse breeding. The foal which his Diamond had had the year before Stroxton Tom was born was by Bar None, but never turned out any good. He was castrated and, if still alive in 1903, was pulling loads through city streets.

Since all four sons were assembled to parade at the conclusion of the 1903 triumph, this is perhaps the occasion to review the Forshaw family. Tom and his wife had two daughters, Mary and Beatrice. Now responsible for all day-to-day matters, he had become at 37 a man of the strictest self-imposed routine. He rose at five in the morning, put the kettle on while he was shaving, brought a cup to tea to Bessie and was out of the house and across the fields to the stables by 5.45. By then, the horses had already received their first feed. He was home for breakfast at 8.15. The day ended with a final visit to the stables just before he went to bed.

Richard, the cricketing vet and former naughty boy, had married Ethel Laming, daughter of a well-know Spalding auctioneer, and settled down responsibly. They had two children. James IV was four, and as the only grandson

so far, which is why he was so named, the apple of his grandfather's eye. Baby Ethel was two. Richard had now bought a mixed farm at Pinchbeck, where his manager looked after a Shire or two for him. Unfortunately, a few months after this great London Show, while he was on his veterinary round one summer afternoon, his pony stumbled and fell. He was tipped out on his head. He said afterwards that he had never lost consciousness, but took a little while to recover.

Fig. 20 Richard the vet on the steps at Hillside, his brother Jim's house.

Jim (James III) was 29 and had been for some long while a frequent caller at Carlton vicarage. The Rev Richard Robinson, who had put Colonel Craig in his place when asked to demote the newcomer James Forshaw in church, was now 67 but Jim did not really come to see him. Having no children of their own, the Robinsons had adopted his young half-sister Maggie. She had been twelve and Jim thirteen when they first met. He was sorry for her because she often had to push Mrs Robinson in a wheel chair, but after he finished his schooling at Bruges, he fell in love with her and they were married this same year, 1903. They moved into Hillside, a new house in the neighbouring village of Sutton-on-Trent.

Like their sister Margaret Blackhurst in Lancashire, Mary and Agnes were now both married – Mary to Robert Atkinson of the Hall Farm at Clarborough near Retford and Agnes, her father's amanuensis in his brief reminiscences, to a Mansfield builder, James Vallance. The baby of the family, William, had just qualified as a doctor.

We must just briefly visit the 1904 show – for four reasons. First, it was the biggest one ever held, the total of 862 animals passing the 1902 record by two. Growth beyond that point was prohibited by the London County Council and the Fire Brigade which both feared the possibility of a holocaust. Secondly, it is only fair to say that Lord Rothschild's Birdsall Menestrel, twice marginally defeated by Stroxton Tom, won the supreme championship. Thirdly, Capstone Harold won the short-legged class (36 present) for the fourth successive year. This too was a record, but the championship could scarcely be expected of him. It was virtually impossible to reach the absolute top of the tree without an extra hand to stand on. Finally, that good old stalwart Nailstone Coeur-de-Lion, which had not been brought to London in the four previous years, reappeared now to win his second first prize, heading the 51 big stallions at the age of nine. This was a typical Forshaw ploy. Having already won a first prize once, he had been kept out of the way during the interval, so that other Carlton horses would not have to compete against him.

Visits to Carlton by such reporters as possessed a vocabulary wide enough to describe so many stallions without repeating their adjectives were now commonplace. This year it was the County Gentleman, whose representative coined the expression "three-ton horse" for Wiggenhall Spartan. This creature was indeed elephantine, but the phrase was a little fanciful, being intended to mean the horse was fit to pull a three-ton load. Among his other notable contributions to equine jargon was his comment on a son of Stroxton Tom called Fourhundred Bonnie Boy, who had "the size and strength of a whale".

Richard, who had almost forgotten about his accident the year before, received a sharp reminder one evening when, with his elbow on the table, his hand suddenly dropped, out of control. He had incipient paralysis of the brain and the speed of his deterioration now became alarming. He suffered periods of violence. He started buying stallions in a reckless manner, scarcely knowing what he was doing. His practice had to be given up, and he was brought back to Carlton. Ethel, whose father had just died suddenly, was given the only

Fig. 21 Jim's first two children, Richard II and Agnes. The card on the horse's neck reads "First Prize, Thorne and District Agricultural Society."

available accommodation for herself and her children, one of three workers' cottages at Barrel Hill, Sutton. Then he had to be sent to The Lawns, a private asylum at Lincoln. Meanwhile his father was increasingly racked by arthritis, and diabetes was wasting him.

After two more firsts for Carlton in 1905, 1906 came within an ace of being something very special. Tom produced four which stood top of their classes – Royal Duke (short legs), Present King II (big), Bay Thumper (old – he was 12) and, unusually for the Forshaws, the mare Sussex Bluegown. This offered the possibility of bettering even the 1903 record. Could the firm possibly end up with both championships as well as four firsts?

Present King was a perfect example of the Forshaw gift for spotting a potential winner – not as a foal this time but in the guise of an adult hitherto disregarded by anyone else. Less than twelve months earlier he had been plucked from obscurity in the middle of the Lincolnshire Wolds, already six years old and rough. Now he beat the winners of all the other classes, including the King's four-year-old Ravenspur as well as his own two stable mates, to win the championship. Joseph Phillipson, who had bred and sold him, wished he had taken Mr Forshaw's advice to join the Society. Breeders of the champion stallion and mare were now eligible to receive a gold medal as well as £10 – if they were members.

What about Sussex Bluegown? Could she make it a championship double? Now six, she too had come from nowhere at even shorter notice, having been acquired only the previous autumn. For her breeder, Thomas Luckin of

Pulborough, she had won a prize or two, but never outside Sussex or Surrey – inferior shire-breeding counties of whose precise whereabouts those who lived north of the Thames affected to be ignorant. For example, just before being bought by Tom, she had won a second prize at Reigate, in the tenant farmers' class and as one of a pair of mares. Now she won the championship and most self-appointed experts in the Hall thought the judges had not had much trouble in making up their minds. What had been done to convert her into the best mare in all England only Tom and his father and Jim and the staff knew.

The press correspondents went into such ecstacies at the triumph of the unknown heroine that they almost forgot that Present King II was an equally unknown hero. They wrote of her majestic bearing, her enormous weight and (for a mare) her great height of 17.1 hands. They exclaimed that she had "knocked on the head the theory that good Shires cannot be bred south of the Thames." Earl Beauchamp who specialised in grey Shires at Madresfield in Worcestershire paid the firm 510 guineas for her. No one had ever heard what Mr Luckin had been happy to accept only six months before. But still, there was the breeder's £10 and gold medal to look forward to, because he had been a member of the Shire Horse Society for fourteen years.

However, the poor chap never received anything. Nor were James Forshaw & Sons allowed to keep their winnings. There was a new show rule that no senior mare could have a prize if she was barren at the time. Bluegown had pretty certainly been in foal on her arrival at Carlton, but she never produced it. She had presumably aborted the embryo in a field one night, watched by a crafty and hungry fox who had removed all the evidence. So, a couple of months after the Show her honours were withdrawn and awarded to Princess Beryl, the reserve champion. Lord Rothschild was given the three cups, gold medal and £15 cash. The breeder's medal and money went to Major-General Sir Henry Ewart, GCVO, KCB in Essex. Luckin had been especially unfortunate because he had tried so hard. Bluegown had been sent all the way to Carlton for Nailstone Coeur-de-Lion to get the foal that never was. What is more, she had had a grey colt in 1905 and later was a regular breeder for Earl Beauchamp. The one year she missed was when the judges chose her as the best mare in England.

A few months after Bluegown's disqualification, Tom unearthed another hidden mare, five years old and working on a Lincolnshire farm only twenty miles away. He enquired her parentage and was told that her sire was the firm's Southgate Honest Tom, which had been travelling the Gainsborough district in 1900. Though it had never appeared at shows, this stallion was one of the finest stock horses in the land and was highly prized by James, who vowed that it should never be sold while he was alive. Tom also learned that , although eligible, the mare had never been entered in the stud book. He bought her on the spot, almost literally out of the shafts.

On returning home, he announced that he had bought as good a mare as What's Wanted had been a stallion. James refused to listen to such rash talk. When she arrived, he went out to have a look and said he could not see any reason for the comparison. Poor man, he could not see anything much, for his diabetes had already made him almost blind. Six months later, belatedly registered in the book as 52340 Stolen Duchess, the new acquisition made her first-ever appearance in any ring at the 1907 London Show itself – and became champion of the 243 females in the Hall. James himself had rarely exhibited mares, but Tom at the first opportunity had now really accomplished what seemed to have been achieved the year before. And William Harpham, her breeder, had taken his advice and joined the Shire Horse Society just in time to qualify for his gold medal and tenner.

At any one moment, there were nowadays just over a hundred stallions at Carlton, though there was much coming and going, because many were destined for export. With the United States, trade in Shires had been re-established since the economic recovery there after the turn of the century. But it was now a smaller and choicer market in which only a few expert and trusted suppliers did well and only good stallions were acceptable. Old James's policy of always aiming to enhance his reputation was paying rich dividends.

Southgate Honest Tom had to be shot in December. He was thirteen. There were two more firsts for Carlton the following February, in the classes in which James had always specialised. Glen Royal II stood at the head of the short-legged brigade and Bay Thumper again won the veterans' class, at the age of 14. Exactly four weeks after the close of the Show, on 27th March 1908, James died, in his 68th year. In his day there was no way of controlling diabetes.

Those people, great and small, who paid tribute to his deeds managed between them to present a fair picture of his contribution to the improvement of heavy draught horses at home and abroad. "He educated the public," wrote one, "as to what a Shire should be, particularly as to feet, pasterns and legs." Another commented on his "genius at picking out the one foal, perhaps standing near the bottom of a long line, that would grow into excellence and his genius at spotting a good horse in bad condition and worse surroundings." A third referred to his "incredible memory for pedigrees and the faults and virtues of the animals that figured in them." In the words of a fourth, he "increased the prestige of the Shire at home and inspired the confidence of buyers abroad. One American gentleman was bold enough to address a telegram to 'Forshaw England'." A fifth said, "He was universally respected. His show-ring successes, though so many, were invariably well received." This was high praise. Not every man at the top of a tree has no enemies on the lower branches. Yet another remarked that he "delighted in helping the small struggling farmer to get into the line of a true Shire". For all his constant striving after success and perfection, this last observation, more than any other, saw into the heart of the man.

9. Two Sons

Following James's death, there was an exchange of homes. Tom and Bessie took over the Stud House and Mary Ann, now 73, moved to Scotfield with £500 a year and the right to enjoy the house during her lifetime, after which it would belong to Agnes Vallance. The Tuxford farm, which had been let, was now the property of Mary Ann junior, Mrs Atkinson. When poor Richard died in the Lincoln asylum on 27th October, three months after his fortieth birthday, it was a merciful release not only for him but for Ethel and her two children, and the rest of the family. (Alcoholic Uncle George, had he been still about, would have been an embarrassment to the two teetotal brothers, though stud workers had treated him tolerantly enough.)

One further death, four days before Christmas this same year, requires notice. Sir P Albert Muntz, Conservative M P for the Tamworth Division of Warwickshire and old James's senior by nearly two years, had played a key role in the spread of pedigree Shiredom. He was par excellence its apostle and expounded the gospel everywhere. No gentleman's sale of horses was complete unless Sir Albert took the luncheon chair, no dinner memorable if he were not the principal speaker. He was renowned for his vast store of coarse anecdotes, and when he had set the company roaring he would turn to his message of salvation for lost and depressed farmers. His favourite peroration contained the rhetorical question, "Why do I breed Shires?" And he always answered, amid rapturous applause, "Because it *pays* me to do so." His Dunsmore stud near Rugby, helped not a little by the wealth which had poured upon his head from the 'Muntz Metal' patented by his father in 1832, had won a phenomenal number of London awards, especially in recent years, and its total, now standing at 175, had caught and passed even the Forshaws' 164 – though if we were to grade them all on a points system he would be found not to have done anything like so well, and the championship had always eluded him.

At Nailstone, the widowed Annie Barrs had died at the age of 51 in 1903 and so young Warner was master of his own destiny; not a very capable one, as he was drinking more and more and already far too much. Nevertheless, the Barrs total was now 104 with Lord Rothschild, on 102, remorselessly creeping closer year by year. The Earl of Ellesmere had slackened off and his score was 90.

On 9th January 1910 Tom received a letter from Emilio N Casares who wrote, "I want you to come out to Buenos Aires and judge Shires on 3rd June. Now I am asking you the first of anyone. Don't mention this to anyone yet please, excepting your brother." The occasion was to be a very grand one – an International Agricultural Exhibition organised by the Sociedad Rural Argentina to celebrate the centenary of the revolution against Spanish rule. So, leaving

Jim to cope with the busiest time of the year, Tom sailed on RMS Oravia on 5th May. Bessie made certain he was well organised for the trip. She gave him a list of what she had put in his cabin trunk: "21 dress shirts, 1 print shirt, 1 dickie, 2 doz dress collars, 2 doz day collars, 2 doz dress ties, 5 pairs cuffs. Dinner suit, dress suit, morning suit, grey suit, striped suit. Shirts collars and cuffs, ties waistcoats and dinner trousers under tray: coats and trousers in tray." He could not go wrong.

Two days out of Liverpool and convalescing from seasickness while the ship lay at La Rochelle, he heard of the King's death. A few days later he was fit enough to sing a few songs in a concert. The captain also appointed him choirmaster. "Had to select chants and hymns for tomorrow, Whitsunday," he wrote to Bessie. "I had nearly all the saloon passengers and several 2nd saloon in for choir practice at 10.30 this morning, and they did well." At 3.30 the following morning he got up to see Halley's comet, "a beautiful sight". He added, "I'm playing in a cricket match on Monday at St Vincent where we call for coal. I was in good form at practice and was the only one they couldn't get out. I hope to do as well on Monday." As he made no later reference to the game, one might assume that he did not.

The steerage people, about four hundred of them, were "nearly all foreign, a rough-looking party, scarcely fit for an ordinary person to be amongst". But they included an English woman and her little son. Tom organised a whip-round among the saloon passengers, who paid for the transfer of the unfortunates to second class. "She seemed a very superior young woman and we as Britishers thought it our duty to act up to it."

He was elected chairman of the committee for sports day – chalking the pig's eye, deck quoits, croquet, egg-and-spoon, whistling race, potato race and so on – and won a few prizes himself. He trained his choir to sing better still the second Sunday, played in several on-deck cricket matches ("gave the officers a good drubbing, but it's difficult when the ship is rolling and pitching"), sang *True till death* at a second concert, played a lot of bridge, and was already homesick. "I have the photo stuck up in my cabin, so see you all every time I go in."

He reached Buenos Aires on Sunday 29th May, was met by his doctor brother William and on the Wednesday started judging three breeds of horse. The Suffolk set him no problem, because there was only one – a six-year-old imported stallion called Rendlesham Barzillai. There were 46 Clydesdales. The Shire classes mustered 69 altogether, 50 of them stallions and colts. The fourteen senior stallions, all but two imported, included Hargrave Harold, *nacido* 1902, who was "head and shoulders above the others", as he explained in his official report. This was a son of the famous old Capstone Harold and had in fact himself won a couple of London prizes for J Forshaw & Sons before being sold to his present *expositor*, Miguel A Martinez de Hoz. If this was potentially embarrassing to the judge, he did not find it so, because it never occurred to him to do other than choose the best horse. The same owner also exhibited the best of the fifteen three-year-olds, King's Sort (*criador*, Bernard Wall, Coleshill,

Fig. 22 The front cover of La Ilustración shows Tom (right) contemplating King's Sort in the ring at La Exposición Rural Argentina, June 1910

Inglaterra). Tom reported that he was "one of the most perfect horses of the breed that ever entered a ring", and had no hesitation in making him champion, entitled to the *medalla de oro* offered by the Shire Horse Society of the United Kingdom of Great Britain and Ireland.

Eighteen of the 21 two-year-olds were Argentine-bred, and Tom did not think much of them. He awarded only one prize, and that to an English colt. The mare classes followed the same pattern. The champion was Inskip Rose, a daughter of his late father's special old favourite Southgate Honest Tom. She belonged to Benjamin Gimenez Pax, like Martinez de Hoz a staunch member of the English as well as of the Argentinian Shire Horse Societies.

Señores F de Lestapis, judge of the 64 Percherons and Victor Even, who had 24 Boulonnais to examine but was not faced even with one Belgian, were so infected by their English colleague's enthusiasm for King's Sort that, when the three met to select the overall champion of the show, they were of one mind. Tom was fêted throughout as a sort of minor deity. In a letter to Bessie, he wrote modestly to "tell Jim that my judging bears all criticism, which they are not afraid to express in this part of the world".

He was intrigued by the fact that in all breeds ages were divided at 1st July instead of the northern hemisphere's 1st January. Argentinian-bred animals were all foaled in the period September-December. This resulted in a colt foaled in September 1907 and an imported one foaled in June 1908 being in the same class, as two-year-olds. He had examined horses born in every month of the year except July, August and January.

During the next two weeks he was lavishly entertained. One of the highlights was a visit to Señor Martinez de Hoz' estancia not far from Buenos Aires. "We went in sleeper carriages about 300 miles, drove in motor cars all day looking at stock in hundreds, and back again by train at night. Here 8 am. His is a grand big place." Another trip was to stay a few days with William and his Irish wife Mabel (née Young), who had brought out Miss Birchnell, a nurse from Sutton, to run a nursing home at Corrientes. "By boat about 370 miles, but it took us two days to get here owing to fog. The last 120 miles we did in the guard's van of a cattle train." He was shocked by his brother's descriptions of Argentinian life. For example, if there were two men fighting in the street, it was certain that William would find them later sitting side by side in his surgery. As long as each had drawn blood, William said, they were content. Thomas thought this foreign behaviour most extraordinary.

He had been in Argentina seventeen days when he wrote again to Bessie that "I'm anxious to hear of Newark and Notts Shows. In ten more days I shall have my head and feet turned towards you, my love. I shall be delighted when I step on shore in Old England, and something very peculiar will have to happen to persuade me to leave it any more. William has plenty of work and is highly respected. I am sure he will do real well, but give me dear Old England. I should think I am the only man out in these parts who doesn't have a revolver." He wrote that he hoped to dock at Southampton on 15th July about noon and to arrive in London at four. He asked Bessie if she could meet him at the Great Northern Hotel at King's Cross, so that they could travel home together on the 6.05 and reach Carlton at 8.36. He had already worked it all out.

And so at last he did sail home, in fine voice to sing *Jack's the Boy* as well as *True till Death* at a *concerto* on RMS Araguaya. He landed at the time expected, ten weeks and a day after his departure. His return home with Bessie, who had met him as suggested, was celebrated by every available Forshaw assembled on the lawn and cheering.

He told the reporter from the ever faithful Lincoln Gazette that 'Boonus Airs', with one and a quarter million people and any amount of traffic, was very like the East End of London. "They are desperate for heavy horses, and the railways are absorbing them right and left. The Argentinian horse is a light animal and it takes four generations to grade them up. Even then it is uncertain whether they'll turn out Shires or nags. But at one estancia where they have been taking stallions from us for twenty-five years" (he was referring to Señor Martinez de Hoz) "I saw a thousand draught horses, all heavy, graded. They still need our stallions out there."

That autumn Jim had time to make another of his frequent visits to France. In the United States the demand for heavy horses was now largely concentrated on the Percheron. Fluent in French as in German, he was of course an ideal agent for their purchase. He brought an enormous number back to England for immediate re-export, and loaded 125 on to one deck of a ship in a single day. An appreciative American presented him with a digital watch, which was a great curiosity, though not so accurate as a proper one with hands.

The brothers were alike in appearance but in temperament, and to some extent in their skills, different. Perhaps it was this that made them ideal partners. Tom was a stoic, always in control of his emotions, imperturbable, neither

Fig. 23 Jim's son Richard as a boy at prep school.

depressed nor exhilarated by success or failure; a man who never shouted or swore. He was a horseman born, and one cannot imagine his becoming anything else. Jim, though scarcely mercurial, was more variable and could produce an impressive flow of strong language if the occasion required it. Though he had become a good horseman, he was a better businessman. He was a sterner father than Tom. For example, his eldest child Richard, now six years old, put up his stocking a second time on Boxing Day with the announced intention of getting more presents from Father Christmas. He awoke in the morning and tipped it out on the bed. It had been filled with lumps of coal. Tom, who had also added a son, another Thomas, to his two daughters, would probably have taught the lesson in a different way, by a low-key but crushing little lecture. All in all, whereas Tom was completely fulfilled by his work, one might wonder whether Jim (though it is to be doubted whether he ever thought about it) would have been more at home in academic surroundings. Not only had he been well educated, but he was very well-read. In this he had little in common with the vast majority of horsemen who, then as later, were not inclined to read a book at all unless it was about horses.

In 1911, Nailstone Coeur-de-Lion put in his fourteenth season on the Carlton staff. He had won two firsts in London and for four years in succession his progeny had topped the auction sale prices there. He had also twice been champion at the Peterborough Spring Stallion Show, now second in importance only to the breed show itself. At sixteen, he was still very fit and fertile when Tom unexpectedly sold him for a tidy sum to James Fisher of Exning, near Newmarket. Fisher was setting up as a proprietor of stallions, which he did by the simple method of purchasing seven two-year-olds from Carlton, including a son of the old horse which he called Kirtling Coeur-de-Lion. Perhaps he bought the father to show the young ones what to do.

This same year, the Board of Agriculture introduced a voluntary scheme to inspect stallions for freedom from hereditary disease. This was a long overdue attempt to discourage the use of 'scrub' horses by providing the owners of sound ones with official certificates which they could wave before the eyes of mare-owners. But all the leading professionals in the pedigree stallion business, and all the great amateurs except old Abraham Grandage of Bramhope ignored this well-intentioned offer.

Two years later, however, Tom and Jim completely changed their mind, and others quickly followed suit. The cause was another Board of Agriculture innovation, the Improvement of Livestock Scheme, which provided for a modest subsidy to hiring societies if they used approved stallions. To qualify, a horse had either to pass the Government examination or have a good honours degree in the form of an award at the London Shire Show, where of course he came under the eyes and hands of the successors to Professor Pritchard and the appropriately named Professor Axe. New hiring societies sprang up in areas where everything had been left to chance before, and all the big names in the stallion business now supported the voluntary vetting scheme. Government interference was one thing: Government money another.

10. War and Post-War

At the beginning of August 1914 the British Army had 25,000 horses and mules of all types. In less than a fortnight a further 140,000, many of them heavy draught horses, had been recruited by compulsory purchase. Farmers too needed extra ones to bring new land under cultivation and town operators and the railways could not manage if theirs were reduced in number. So breeding for victory was urgent, though in fact the first war-foals could not be conceived until 1915 and born in 1916, and would not be fit for military or urban service before 1921. Although hostilities were not expected to last as long as that, this point seems to have occurred to no one.

The war brought Dr William and his wife home from Corrientes to the London Hospital, where for four years he was to perform an annual average of two thousand operations. In November 1914, the death of Sir Walter Gilbey at the age of 83 symbolised for horsemen the end of the era, which the outbreak of hostilities had shattered. He had done more than any other man to promote the welfare of horses and, as founder of the London Cart Horse Parade in 1885, of the urban toiler in particular. Nor was he universally called "the horseman's friend" for no reason.

As the 1915 season began, 36 stallions were sent out from Carlton, the same number as the year before. Most had been hired by local societies but, of those on 'independent' routes, five went to Lancashire, celebrating the centenary of great-grandfather's first stallion in the Fylde. A further thirteen remained at home to serve visiting mares or to depart at a moment's notice to relieve or assist a colleague in trouble. The number of two-year-old colts on trial this year is impossible to ascertain.

Lord Rothschild, unique in the professional way his amateur stud was operated, died on 31st March 1915. Warner Barrs drank himself progressively to his death on 23rd November a few months after his 34th birthday, having dissipated a stallion enterprise that his father had made no less successful than that of James Forshaw. The Nailstone stud was no more. All he left after him were three little sons, three little daughters and their 32 year-old mother Agnes. Fortunately she soon married the elderly George Johnson, a widower of Barton-in-the-Beans.

We are now entering the period of which there survive personal memories not only of the Forshaw horses but of their employees and customers. It is therefore right to give these people at last the attention they deserve. Since this cannot be done within a strictly chronological framework, they must have chapters of their own. In order to accommodate these, we now have to review the events from one year to the next more rapidly than before.

In 1916 experienced stallion leaders were released for the first time from military duties during the breeding season. Carlton had several of these and they were supplemented by old men brought out of retirement to totter once again round their old routes where mares were covered, which in peace time would not have been offered to the stallion at all. At home a depleted staff was coping with a greatly increased workload. For example, there was an average of nearly seventy geldings coming in every month in order to be sent out again to the Army Remount Depots as soon as they were passed for fitness.

The human population of the country had been accurately counted at ten-year intervals ever since 1801, but no one had had any real idea how many horses there were. Those which worked on farms had been included in the Agricultural Returns to the Board of Trade ever since 1869, but even these partial figures had long been suspect. Those farmers who believed in the freedom of the individual tended not to answer the question properly if at all and civil servants in these cases preferred to make a guess rather than seek trouble. Just briefly, in the four years 1870-1873, non-agricultural horses were taxed and so by adding the two categories together it was possible to get some fair notion of the whole. When as a result of furious and prolonged outcry the tax was abolished, we returned to ignorance on this matter. However, in view of the vital importance of horses in the war effort, an Order was made on 17th April 1917, by the Quartermaster-General to the Forces under Regulation 15 of the Defence of the Realm Act, requiring a complete census on the 21st of that month. It may be thought, in retrospect, that this good idea was somewhat belated. However that may be, the police did all the work and sent the forms in to the Board of Trade. The total number of horses in Great Britain was found to be 2,079,122, of which 61.4% were draught animals. Of the latter, 787,175 were classified as 'agricultural' and the 'trade' horses were subdivided into 'heavy' (247,304) and 'light or medium' (242,919). In addition, on 31st August the Army had 869,931 horses and mules, although it had already lost 256,204.

The Royal Agricultural Hall was now taken over for assembling aircraft. The 'London' Show in 1918, therefore, became a 'Newmarket' Show and was restricted by Government instruction to stallions only. Rickford Coming King, ten years old, won the championship for Carlton. By the time the war ended, the Army had purchased 1,212,177 horses and mules and 529,564 of them had been destroyed, posted as missing or rendered unfit for service. The French army had lost more than this, even by 1st October 1917.

It was doubtful if the Hall would be vacated in time for the 1919 Show, which for a second time was therefore held at Newmarket with stallions only. Again the championship went to a Carlton horse, the four-year-old Generosity. He turned out to be a disaster for the Forshaws and, in making a mockery of the show system for selecting stallions for service, an embarrassment to the Shire Horse Society. This was especially unfortunate at a time when the excellent Percheron breed, introduced from France in the middle of the war, appeared likely to set up a serious challenge to the English horse. The Council of the newly-formed British Percheron Horse Society, under the presidency of the Earl of Lonsdale, mostly comprised 'new' people – nine army officers, two other earls, a baronet and four esquires – and the publicity they were achieving caused apoplexy amongst stout Shire men, though a few of the less stout and the more open-minded were already showing some interest in the immigrant breed.

The 1920 Show, in London again, was one of those at which Carlton could not compete because Jim had been asked to judge. It was the most remarkable of all time. On the third day, an estimated five thousand people stood in dense fog and blocked the roads outside the Hall because the place was crammed full and the doors had been locked. A roar of approval from the lucky ones inside signalled that the King's homebred Field Marshal V had won the championship. When it was announced that His Majesty was the first man since 1901, the year of his glorious grandmother's death, to be both breeder and owner of the champion of either sex, patriotic postwar enthusiasm exploded into even more vociferous cheering. Never had the London judges proved so universally popular – and wise. Only Percy Toone from Hinkley, who had kept shouting out in favour of the winner of the senior cup, F W Cope's Blaisdon Draughtsman, had the nerve to express any displeasure at the result. Mr Cope of course sportingly hid his disappointment behind a smile and cordially shook hands with His Majesty, who then shook the judges' hands very cordially. Draughtsman had also just missed the championship the year before, when the Forshaw's Generosity had been preferred (Poor Fred Cope was destined to have a thin time in the early Twenties. In 1921, the King's horse was champion again, and Draughtsman again runner up. Then he lost most of his nose in an accident. Then he was thrown out of the Shire Horse Society for substituting one mare for another at a minor show. Eventually, however, he was reinstated and ended up as a member of the panel of judges).

When the travelling season began in 1920, leaders had to be briefed to carry with them at all times their stallion's licence, because the Horse Breeding Act 1918, making the Ministry's veterinary inspection compulsory, had come into operation on the first day of the year. It was now illegal for any stallion to serve any mare, except at home, unless he had a permit to do so. Officious policemen kept watch for entire horses on the road, and their owners or attendants found it useless to claim that they were only going for a walk. Any stallion who set foot outside his own premises was deemed to be plying for service. Many men regarded this as yet one more example of depriving Englishmen of their liberties – necessary perhaps in a war but intolerable in peace time. However, since stallions operated in ones, anything in the nature of a mass demonstration was out of the question. In any case, the chief stallion owners were in support of the law. It would improve the standard of breeding – and tend to increase their custom. Compulsory veterinary inspection, following belatedly after the stud book, London Show and the hiring society movement, was the fourth and final contribution to the general improvement of the English cart horse.

In this first year, application was made for licences in England and Wales on behalf of 2520 pedigree Shire stallions – and 262 (10.4%) were refused. Twenty out of 108 non-pedigree Shires were turned down. If we include Clydesdales in England, Suffolk and Percherons, 3,019 licences were granted

– no less than 51 of them to the Forshaw brothers. The second census, taken that year, showed 1,231,469 draught horses in England and Wales, of which 868,959 were of the heavy sort, three years old or more. Great Britain as a whole then had a little over two million horses of all types.

The war had been a bonanza for breeders and dealers and the boom continued in Britain right through most of 1920 because civilian demand at home to replace those horses that had been kept at work too long was high, while France, Belgium and other western European nations were desperate to get anything that could stand on four legs and pull. The fighting had left these countries almost destitute of horsepower. At Carlton the coming and going of work horses to and from the Army had of course ceased and life returned to normality. Even so, 840 horse boxes came into the siding that year and 840 went out – stallions about their lawful business, mares to be served and go home, or bought and sold. March King was let to the Crewe Society for £1,000 and was already booked in advance to the Newark Society at £2,000 for 1921.

£2000! Were they mad, round Newark? Even before 1920 ended, there was a slow-down in the horse trade. It was bound to be followed by a terrible slump. The Army had a quarter of a million surplus horses which were being dumped on the market at a carefully controlled rate – 41% of them light draught animals and 17% Shire and other heavy types. People were sure that the internal combustion engine would be able to do things that only horses, helped by a

Fig. 24 Tom outside the Stud House with Thomas junior, the third of his four children and only son.

Fig. 25 Jim and Maggie, photographed by their son Richard on the steps of Hillside.

little steam, had ever done before. This expectation would turn out to be at least premature and would not be fulfilled for another twenty-five years – not only because the farm tractor was temporarily shown to be inefficient, but also because farmers, hurtling downwards from war boom to postwar depression, would soon have no money to buy one.

In the New Year of 1921, Tom's wife Bessie was seriously ill at home and thought to be dying of a burst stomach ulcer. Her cousin Sarah Swift, who for many years had been spending her holidays at Carlton, came to take charge. Probably the most distinguished private nurse that any ordinary person ever had in sickness, she had been matron of Guy's Hospital, founder of the Royal College of Nursing, Matron-in-Chief of the British Red Cross during the war and in 1919 had been created Dame Grand Cross of the British Empire.

At this time Tom junior, now 16, was on holiday from Wellingborough and on the 10th of the month his great friend Rowland Farrow took him and another boy called Bembridge for an unauthorised ride in his father's car, and drove it into a telegraph pole. It was Tom who died. His father, outwardly impassive as he invariably was, could not bring himself to lay the burden of the news on the mother until just before the funeral. He had now to discuss the future of the firm with Jim, for it had been intended that Tom junior would join them on leaving school. What could be the alternative plan? Their late brother's son

James would have been a good choice. He had progressed from spudding thistles at the age of nine to exercising stallions when he was eleven and producing them for prospective customers. The boy had had a natural aptitude for handling horses and they looked huge as they towered over his little frame – but it was too late to think of him. At the outbreak of war, when he was 14, he had gone to live in Newark with his widowed mother and sister, joined the army as soon as he was old enough and was now at University.

Jim had two sons. The fifth child, yet another James, was far too young and so the partners settled on Richard, who was approaching the end of his schooldays at Repton. For the time being it did not occur to them to inform him what he was going to do with his adult life.

The inevitable slump arrived and the 1922 London Show opened amidst the deepest gloom. The number of horses exhibited dropped to exactly 500. Rickford Coming King, the 1918 champion, won first prize among the veterans at the age of fourteen and Colney King 2nd achieved the same distinction in the 'short-legs' class, which had now been won by a Forshaw stallion seventeen times out of a possible thirty-six, with eleven different horses. Roycroft Forest King, which had cost the firm £1,700 to buy in 1919 and had enhanced his worth by winning first prize in 1921, was not shown this year. The brothers put a paper value on him of £250. The tax man thought they were joking and so Jim proposed that, to test the situation, the horse should be sent to Peterborough spring auctions and should be reserved at that figure. He doubted if there would be a buyer. The Inland Revenue graciously conceded the point.

J Forshaw & Sons were among the very few people in the land whose business was entirely dependent on the breeding of cart horses. To reduce their financial risk, a pedigree herd of Friesian cows was established by selecting well-fleshed animals, with a high butter-fat record and paying 800 guineas for a fine South African bull, which they called Carlton Overwinnaar. After the manner of Robert Bakewell, they used him on his own daughters to produce prepotent young bulls for sale to dairy-farmers. In the next few years, they showed that they could succeed at this too, but as things were to turn out their experiment in diversification was not necessary after all.

11. Third Man

Wearing an Eton collar and his prep-school uniform, Richard Forshaw had paid his first visit to the London Show in February 1914, when he was nine and a bit. He saw Uncle Tom judging. He was also taken to the theatre, where Josie Collins sang *The Last Waltz*. At the Great Northern Hotel there was a lift and he had never seen one before. He went up and down so often that his father had to give a big extra tip to the boy who operated it.

At Repton in 1918 one of the other new boys was Michael Ramsey. The headmaster was Geoffrey Fisher, a great friend of his predecessor Dr William Temple, who frequently revisited the school. A rotund man, Temple got a foot on the episcopal ladder in 1921 when he became Bishop of Manchester, and on his next visit got stuck in a door because someone had failed to open the other leaf for him. (This was the only thing for which the younger Reptonians remembered him.) So in later life Richard, always a staunch churchman, was able to claim that he had met three future Archbishops of Canterbury before he was eighteen. A second exact contemporary at school was the future novelist and playwright Christopher Isherwood, who was clever and used to do his Latin prep for him. Richard sometimes used to stay with him and his mother (his father had been killed in the war) and was impressed by the younger brother who knew every bus route in London. It was only later, when Christopher went off the heterosexual rails, that the friendship petered out. Whenever in later years Isherwood's name cropped up, he simply spoke of him as "the poor chap".

Neither his father nor Uncle Tom had had the opportunity to play ball games in their youth and even the uncle after whom he had been named had become a good cricketer in spite of his schooling, not because of it. Richard himself excelled at football and as a batsman and therefore flourished at Repton. Though he was not particularly academic, this helped him to get a place at Christ's College, Cambridge. His mother hoped he would go into the Church, but he thought he was more suited to read Agriculture. However, both aspirations were dashed by his father at the eleventh hour. His education terminated abruptly in July 1922. The school, as a compromise, suggested he should remain for just one more term in order to strengthen the team – Repton being one of the few great public schools to play soccer. But it was not to be and on the first Monday of October, instead of getting his things ready for Cambridge, he reported to the stables at six o'clock. Chapman, the foreman, was busy feeding horses, and said, "The best thing you can do is to get hold of this shovel". One of the men commented, "All that money poured into your education, and you're only doing the same as me".

There were only 402 horses at the 1923 show, the lowest entry since 1887 and less than 47% of the record gathering of 1904. Numbers in the Hall were boosted, however, by introducing 'commercial' classes for geldings or mares in harness with vehicle. These attracted 52 additional entries, but were really rather pointless at a breed show. The Forshaw family rejoiced when Rickford Coming King stood first once again among the veteran stallions to become at fifteen the oldest horse ever to achieve this since the class was instituted in 1895.

The Ministry issued 2120 licences for heavy stallions in England and Wales this year – a drop of almost 30% from 1920. Shires had decreased by 32.9% to 1634 but the Forshaws, swimming against the tide, with the help of their reputation, held 54 licences, three more than at the last count. Clydesdales, mostly in the northern counties, were reduced from 296 to 191 and Suffolks only by ten to 187. The figure for the recent immigrant Percheron had risen from 42 to 47. There were still 61 "others" untouched by over forty years of the pedigree movement.

The breeding season opened in gloom. One society had hired two Carlton horses but sent one back because not enough mares had been nominated. No one seemed anxious to breed foals they could not sell. If the partners had demanded even partial payment they would have run good customers into debt and possible dissolution – and what about all other societies? If they were able to put only fifty mares to the horse when they had budgeted for a hundred or more, they would be asking for a rebate when the season was over. Five stallions died, all in their early prime. Among them was March King, the horse that had been let for £2,000 two years before. He was seven. Richard wondered whether his arrival had brought a blight on the firm.

At the 1924 Show, the veteran stallions class was axed as an economy measure. This was a deplorable decision. To continue it would have given the best possible encouragement to breeders to look for hard-wearing qualities in the sires they used, and in the long term could have helped to persuade towns-people to keep using horses, which (like human labour) were cheap, rather than switch to motors, which were not. The new commercial turnout classes, attracting brewers and other wealthy town owners, paid for themselves, but that was irrelevant. It looked as if the Society was losing faith in its own future.

Not long after the show Mary Ann, faithful supporter of her husband in his early struggles, genial hostess at the Angel and later at Carlton, and now for 16 years the honoured doyenne of a family known throughout the world, died on 15th April, in her 91st year. Mrs Miles, who as Louie Metcalf had been her paid companion for three years and was one who never lost her forthright and honest way of speaking, described her – half a century later – as "the most marvellous person in the world, always kind, always gracious, never ruffled. And she was as pretty as paint." Now the old lady's daughter-in-law Maggie, Jim's wife and mother of Agnes, Margaret, Marian and yet another little James, as well as Richard, was in an advanced state of tuberculosis.

At cricket, the third man position is an odd one, neither glamorous nor specialist. As the stud's third man, Richard was sometimes groom, sometimes office clerk and sometimes Young Mr Forshaw as he learned every part of the business. The more he learned, the more adaptable he had to be. He was a young man with an ease and charm of manner and an attractive speaking voice which enabled him to deputise for uncle or father in anybody's company: and occasions for this grew more frequent, as both his seniors became more and more involved in affairs of the breed society, agriculture in general and other outside activities, which their eminence increasingly made it difficult to avoid. Although not quite 'cradled among horses', he soon proved a sound judge and a good showman. Forshaw employees had never had a chance to exhibit horses in the ring as men did at other establishments. With Richard's arrival, they rarely would in the future. When his mother died the following spring, the officials of a local show kindly agreed to his deputising as judge for his stricken father. The circumstance in which he became, presumably by a long way, the youngest-ever Shire judge was not, therefore, a happy one. The judge of horses, like the referee or umpire, must make his decisions on what he actually sees, not upon what he knows about the competitors. An example of failure to do this occurred later in the year, when the firm exhibited Buckwell Blend and Cippenham Draughtsman at the Yorkshire Show. Draughtsman, which had been let to the Brigg Society, was sure to win and so Richard took him into the ring. His uncle took Blend, which had been on one of the Lancashire routes, to get the very best position he could for him. This confused the judge, who put Tom's horse at the top and 'the boy's' second.

At London in 1926, the parade of prizewinners was headed by Tom, leading the new nine-year-old champion. Lincoln What's Wanted II. Jim led Dogdyke Jonathan, which had won first prize in the short-legged group and Dr Bill the winner of the yearling class, named Co-operation because he was bred by the Scunthorpe Co-op on its Winteringham farm. Richard paraded Maryshall Hero, beaten into second place among the four-year-olds by an ex-Carlton horse sold at a handsome profit six months before. Except for this slight imperfection and for its being a different Richard, this was a repeat of 1903. Nor was it less difficult to achieve, for it was the worst, not the best, which were missing from the Show during the slump. Tom of course had actually shown these four in front of the judges, though Richard had been blooded by exhibiting a three-year-old called Royal Wonder which had little chance of a major honour, but for which he managed to achieve fifth place.

As Young Mr Forshaw, Richard was acceptable anywhere. As an anonymous young man with a cart stallion it might be different. This year he took two horses to Carmarthen. The local hiring society was supplying the grooms, but it was a good idea for a member of the family to be seen at the local parade prior to the season. After a ghastly journey of twenty-one hours, the train arrived at three in the morning. It was pouring with rain. The society's secretary was at the station and they walked the horses to the hotel which had been booked, and stabled them. Gaining admittance for Richard was more difficult. After much hammering at the door, a window was opened and a woman looked out. The secretary explained. She had no sympathy. "The last man who came here with a stallion left nine babies and only eight foals."

The secretary did his best. He appealed both in English and Welsh to her better nature, without success. At last, he produced a vociferous explanation that this was not a groom but Mr Forshaw, a member of the most famous Shire horse family in all the land. Thus mollified, the woman came down and let him in. He was shown to a bed in a sort of dormitory where eight or nine men were already asleep – but he was past caring about that.

Early in May the same year Royal Oak 15th, the stallion hired by the Barnsley and District society, broke down. The General Strike was on but one of the Carlton staff was sent to try to get through with a substitute. A student wearing plus fours drove the train and had to stop at all the level crossings while the volunteer guards opened the gates and then closed them afterwards. When at last they got to Barnsley, the only way of getting the horse out of the station was to walk him through the ticket office. After he was handed over to the groom – a man called Holmes who had never led a horse for Forshaws before, and never did again – getting Royal Oak home for repairs and recuperation was another protracted performance.

Family life now settled down to a routine not to be again seriously disturbed until after the second war. Tom and Bessie's daughters were Mary (now Mrs Graham), Beatrice (Mrs Kirkup) and Mabel, by far the baby of the family. At fourteen, she regarded cousin Richard as a replacement elder brother and an especially kind one, ready to escort her to any party she was old enough to attend.

Fig. 26 Tom, seated beside his mother Mary Ann. Bessie is standing.

Jim's household was run by his corpulent housekeeper, Lily Bell, who helped to maintain a tradition by teaching all the Forshaw girls to make Goosnargh cakes, which she had herself learned to do from old Granny Forshaw. She was very jolly unless anyone caused aggravation, when she became a powerful disciplinary force. Richard of course was also living at home and now acquired a car. Neither of the older men would dream of driving one of these machines and he therefore found himself taking his uncle to see likely young horses in all sorts of places. It was on these excursions that he learned fast, for Tom would always say, "Have a look at that one." After he had made his examination and offered an opinion, Tom would tell him where he was wrong or right, or explain why a seeming fault would rectify itself or a minor weakness become exacerbated in later years.

About this time A B Charlton, secretary of the Shire Horse Society, was making painful efforts to write its jubilee history. The poor man was required to produce draft pages for discussion by the Council in its august chamber at 12 Hanover Square. Most members said little, but he was subjected to so much criticism by Jim that he got into the habit of asking, "Well, what have you found wrong on *this* page?" When Jim got home he would say, "That fellow Charlton, he's always using the word *collate*. He can't get away from it. For him, everything's *collated*. Charlton, though very dignified, loved a joke – but only if he made it himself about someone else. So Jim enjoyed tackling him on such expressions as "the silver lining that appertains to every cloud". When the book appeared, the text occupied 191 pages and the index 46.

On purely social occasions, Jim was not much of a man for small talk. In brothers who closely resemble each other physically and perhaps in basic character, the superficial differences are often unexpected. Tom was the man to keep a party going, as he clearly was when sailing to Argentina. Yet he was the one who was normally most sparing of his words. It was as if he carried nutshells in his pockets to keep them in. His sense of the ridiculous, never flamboyantly expressed as by his father when he pretended to light a cigar at another man's nose, was subtle. When Hugh Sheldon, who later became Jim's son-in-law, exhibited a horse at Collingham Show and it was placed last in a class of fifteen, he was very upset and rushed up to Tom, who had been watching.

"Do you think that was *right*, Mr Forshaw?" he asked.

Tom was silent, deep in thought. At last he gave his well-considered verdict:

"No. I don't think so, Hugh. In my opinion, you should have been placed one higher."

Jim could be equally laconic when he wished. A stranger came into the yard at Carlton and saw a man there.

"Are you Mr Forshaw?" he asked.

"Sometimes."

The stranger was nonplussed. "Who are you at other times?"

"Sometimes I'm Jimmy. At this moment, I'm That Old Bugger. I've just been reprimanding two of the men."

The most noticeable difference between the brothers was revealed in their

Fig. 27 Tom has the umbrella and Jim is wearing gloves

reaction to death. Tom's utter self-control and impassive exterior following his son's fatal accident would probably have held firm if Bessie also had died of her illness at about the same time. Jim on the other hand for long could not disguise his complete devastation on the loss of Maggie.

Neither man drank. Not only had they been indoctrinated with their father's precept about the impossibility, in their line of business and particularly at shows, of drinking sociably with one man without offending another, but they had received object lessons on the perils of drink from old Uncle George, young Warner Barrs and many others. They would speak with awe rather than disapproval of such a man as A-G , who one evening in their presence began to labour under the delusion that he was a duck, and waddled accordingly, as he quacked. On another occasion, put to bed by slightly more sober friends, the poor fellow became convinced that he was a sow giving birth to piglets.

As a class, Shire horse people, usually taciturn, were noted for their ability to hold their drink without becoming aggressive or disgusting: whisky in particular incited them only to innocent if eccentric merriment. There was a saying that, whereas the breeders of the 'new' Percherons were generally teetotal Nonconformist, Shire men tended to be C of E drinkers. However, when Tom or Jim took a glass of sherry on a festival occasion, it would be half a glass, topped up with water, and he thought himself adventurous, declaring that he had become as tight as an owl.

Jim did not smoke. He had tried a cigar when fourteen, as everyone does, but was not tempted again. Tom smoked cigarettes for twenty years, and then gave up because of his singing. He really had an excellent baritone voice, but rarely allowed it to resonate beyond the walls of Carlton church.

All the Forshaws were sports-minded – not so much towards country sports, as one might expect, though Jim was an excellent shot. They all liked ball-games and their notion of a summer Sunday afternoon was to play croquet, then bowls and finish with tennis. Richard, sadly, had too little time available for regular cricket and no longer played soccer. The partners made him work very hard, but his energy was tremendous. After spending the day haymaking he found that tennis, even if he was not free to start until eight o'clock, was a good way to relax. Indoors, Tom loved cards, from bridge to the crudest and noisiest of games. He was also keen on painting, in which his most notable achievement in his young days had been a portrait in oils of Downham Ben, five times a London winner in the Nineties. Christmas was naturally the great occasion for family parties of twenty or thirty people though the Doctor always left on Boxing Day so that he could attend the children's party at the London Hospital. Incidentally, he had now opened a private practice in Surrey at Ewhurst. It was not easy to establish a reputation in that select area. The wealthy were faithful to their old family doctors and the new man had to be content with their servants. He kept a Shire mare or two, but only because his name was Forshaw. A highlight of the year for friends as well as family was the Doncaster races, for which there were big houseparties and, on St Leger evening, a festive dinner party. Tom could rattle off Thoroughbred pedigrees as fluently as Shire ones, or as Jim could discuss the points of a horse in French.

The London Show, as for other leading exhibitors, was another great social event. Four nights in an hotel towards the end of February, with theatres in the evening and the shops for the ladies to tour by day, were a holiday to be anticipated with some pleasure during the dreary post-Christmas weeks. Jim now preferred to stay at the Cora, but Tom always chose the Berners, where one had to dress for dinner. Before he had been there long, he would inevitably say "I'll just go down to the Hall and see if the horses are all right." And Bessie would always need to remind him that they had arranged to dine with this or that family, in case he came back late.

In 1929, a three-year-old called Bold Robin Hood II was required near the end of the season to assist Duke Ashenden on the Isle of Man. Richard took him to Liverpool to put him on the boat so that Graham, the groom, could take delivery at Douglas. Bad weather delayed the sailing. He therefore lodged the horse at the stables of an undertaker called McGuire and stayed two nights

Fig. 28 King George V, who never missed a London Show if he could help it, talking in 1928 to the judges (left to right) Tom Forshaw, Captain A H Clark (Moulton Eaugate, Spalding) and Henry Leggate (Dogdyke, Lincoln).

with the family. This further extended his education, for he was amazed at evening meals to hear the language in which the day's events were discussed. Describing a near-mishap, one of the sons said "The bugger suddenly slipped." Another bugger that looked as if he might slip was Bold Robin Hood himself when at length he could sail. Always an extravagant mover, he seemed about to shoot his legs over the side of the gangway while being loaded up. Richard was glad to get home from that little job.

His first experience of loading a horse for Australia at Tilbury was likewise never forgotten. The journey to King's Cross and the walk to Fenchurch Street were straightforward in so far as leading a stallion through streets crowded with other horses is ever so. But the second train halted at Stratford at about eleven in the morning. There seemed to be a lot of sorting out and shunting, but no forward progress. Eventually peace and tranquillity reigned, but lasted two hours. Wondering whether the horse might miss the boat, he walked back up the track to a signal box to make enquiries. It turned out that everyone had forgotten the box was actually occupied. A locomotive was sent at once.

At the dock-side, Richard was told to take the horse into a container about ten feet square. He did so, but could find nothing to tie him to. They began to shut the doors.

"Hey," said Richard, "I'm getting out."

"Oh no, you're not," was the reply.

There was a slight jerk, hardly noticeable. The horse planted all four feet apart. Richard also did his best, with only two. He thought how mountainously high the ship had looked from the quay. In the complete darkness it was impossible to divine what was happening, if anything, for all seemed still. With the tiniest of bumps, they landed on the deck. The emigrant went calmly to his berth as if he regularly made sky trips with the aid of a crane.

Shows continued to provide as much education as any other activity, and one lesson was an embarrassing one. He was to exhibit a horse which needed a little help with a foot. This had been provided by that standard substitute for horn, gutta percha. On arrival at the showground, he found that this had come out. In a quandary, he had the bright idea of ramming soap into the gap. As he entered the ring, it began to rain heavily. By the time the horses were drawn into line, bubbles were rising from the patched foot. "Would you prefer to withdraw your horse?" the judge politely asked. "I think he is having a little difficulty."

Most people remember their first experience in some activity connected with their work, however trivial. At Richard's earliest major engagement as a judge he had a pair of outstanding geldings before him in a working harness class – the property of a famous brewery. A lump on the leg of one was nothing to prevent him from placing them top, because a working town horse cannot be expected to remain entirely without superficial blemish. Anxious to demonstrate that in spite of his youth he knew what he was about, he drew the man's attention to it.

"Yes, sir, I know. Unfortunately he had a bit of a knock on the way down, and it's brought up that lump."

A year later, judging a different show, he was confronted by the same pair, and the same man. And the same lump. The two men eyed each other and only two sentences were spoken.

"It's taking a fairish time to go down, then."

"Yes sir, it is that."

Appointment to the panel of judges gave Richard a prestige beyond his years. Similarly he was expected at home to assume the mantle of his uncle or father in their absence. Dignity and responsibility rested so lightly on his shoulders that he could shrug them off at will, but he must often have wished that at other times also he could be accepted as an adult. It was typical of late Victorians to expect decorum in a son or nephew while treating him, in his twenties, as still a boy. He continued over the years to drive the old men about the countryside. Tom, perhaps ever mindful that he had lost his son in a road accident, issued a constant stream of instructions and his father was almost as bad. After dark, Uncle would particularly worry about the headlights. "Dip," he would never fail to say when he saw an oncoming car. The inevitability of this was irritating enough, but the certain knowledge that it would be followed by a countermanding "Switch" was worse. One needed the Forshaw control of the emotions to withstand it.

On one long journey home both men, sitting side by side on the back seat, kept up a running commentary. Approaching St Neots, Tom said, "Slow down, Richard. You're speeding". Later his father said, "Speed up a bit. We don't want to be on the road all night." They were approaching a humpback bridge and Richard pressed his foot on the accelerator. When they landed, he looked in the mirror to watch both old buffers struggling to pull their bowler hats up from round their ears. He grinned to himself and the rest of the drive was completed in silence.

In 1932 Tom became President of the Shire Horse Society, an office held by members of the Royal family three times, by dukes three times, earls seven, barons thirteen, baronets and members of the landed gentry nineteen and industrialists of a superior sort six times. The only agriculturalists had been A H Clark in 1922 and Fred Griffin (1926), both farming immense acres in the Fens and breeding from their numerous pedigreed mares. No President, unless of royal or perhaps ducal rank, could confer further distinction upon the Society by accepting office. The honour was transmitted in the opposite direction and was immediately recorded in the next Who's Who. Nor was it a sinecure. The Society had no chairman of its Council other than the President, and the late King Edward VII, when Prince of Wales, had carried out these duties with verve in 1886 and 1899.

Tom was an uncompromising opponent of the proposal made at this time to forge a cautious link with the old enemy the Clydesdale Horse Society, whose breed, if not identical to the Shire as it nearly was in Lawrence Drew's time, was at least its nephew. The idea was, by permitting limited and controlled crossbreeding, to clean up the over-hairy legs of the Shire and give it a smarter action and to provide the Clydesdale with the substance and power which it had been losing. He argued that any necessary modification of the English horse could be achieved from within, without wrecking breeders' calculations by the importation of blood which had been kept entirely distinct for about fifty years.

In a BBC radio programme on 28th February 1934, he debated the matter with Tom Fowler whose former employer Lord Rothschild would have been outraged if he had been alive to hear his heresies. No stallions, even those of Carlton, had been huger, heavier or hairier than those of Tring Park. The script survives but it would be embarrassing to quote, for it reveals only the puerile standard of broadcasting at that time. In any case, the dispute was virtually over, the Forshaw point of view having prevailed in England. As it takes two to make an agreement, the proposal for a new horse was a dead duck. Anyone determined to mix bloods would have to pull his hat over his eyes, turn up his coat collar and lead a stallion across the border at dead of night, and then combine with others in committing perjury when signing pedigree papers.

Jim was also honoured in 1935 when elected President of the National Horse Association. This had been established in 1922, with an initial grant of £100 from the Shire Horse Society, to enable all sections of the horse industry to battle together with their increasingly numerous common problems – slippery road surfaces designed for cars but dangerous for horses, the anti-docking lobby, unfair entertainment tax levied on breed and agricultural shows, abolition of railway concessions, and so on. On the formation of the Institute of the Horse for the encouragement of riding two years later, the Association had concentrated on promoting the harness horse and employed a parliamentary agent to monitor all bills with anti-horse implications. Surprisingly, that very modern man the Prince of Wales, who was not interested in horses, became its Patron in 1930. Jim took office at a particularly difficult time. More and more companies and local authorities which had mechanised their transport were now actually selling their lorries and reverting to horse-haulage. However, in Leslie Hore-Belisha, the new Minister of Transport in Baldwin's National Government, freedom faced a ruthless opponent, who was banning horses from Regent and Oxford Streets and uttering all manner of threats about what he would do next. Jim and the Association fought furiously, basing their arguments on the statistics of traffic jams caused by motors, not horses, produced by an army of vigilant researchers led by Major General Sir John Moore. Fortunately, in 1937 Neville Chamberlain transferred Hore-Belisha to what horsemen considered a more appropriate post as War Minister.

The slight revival of the working horse population in towns had prompted some optimism among breeders. The number of heavy stallion licences had reached its nadir in 1928, when only 1033 were issued. A steady annual increase in the following years brought the figure to 1868 in 1938.

Meanwhile, on 18th January 1936, Richard had met Ida Caraher, in circumstances more reminiscent of his uncle's first sight of Bessie than those which had led to his father's marriage to Maggie. Some years before, Ida had been out walking with her father, a doctor, in the fields near their home in County Louth when, as she opened a gate for him, he dropped dead. This left her mother short of money, though she had just enough for her son Edward to complete his medical studies. They moved to a little house near Dublin and Ida, who was now sixteen, left school and had one or two secretarial jobs until the family left Ireland for Worksop, where Edward doctored the miners.

Ida began to figure increasingly in Richard's diary. For example, 25th November: "Went to Ida's. Car smashed up." Nine days later, he proposed – having of course obtained permission of her mother, who had said, "If she can't get an Irishman, you'll have to do." With such a blessing, no more flattering to her daughter than to him, they married on 9th September 1937 in the slack time of the Carlton year and moved into Grove House, a large Victorian villa in Sutton-on-Trent.

Like those of many who bother to keep one at all, Richard's personal diaries consist of random and apparently inconsequential jottings, intended simply as aides-memoir of dates. Yet, to the outsider who is sufficiently curious and unmannerly as to pry into them, their trivia, frequently ignoring the great national and international news of the day, are oddly revealing, since we all have to go about our private affairs, however earth-shattering the events of the outside

Fig. 29 Richard leaning against his Hillman Minx outside the house.

world may be. It might therefore be excusable to look at a few entries made in 1939. 13th January: "Finished what cigarettes I had left and stopped smoking." 14th: "Not smoking." 8th February: "Carmarthen SHS got Statesman on price and they pay all exes bar rail. (Richards young, Roderick secretary stout, Williams dark and cross-eyed, Jones tall)." 19th March: "Took Thompson round to see his stopping places. Ida did not come – making marmalade. Fetched Father home." 1st August: "School, gas class. Bedford SHS have Carlton Primate on offer 1940." 1st September (a Friday): "Some rain. Father and Uncle shooting. Did first turn of duty in police office 5-9 am. Saw about milking machine." 2nd: "Duty in police office. 48 cows 4 unit 1 spare pail including engine £162-16-0, stainless steel units £20 extra. Each unit two complete sets of liners." 3rd: "Milking in afternoon. Anthony and Agnes with father for tea."

At tea with his wife, father and sister and her husband, the new milking machine no doubt came under discussion. We can assume too, that they talked about the announcement, made in church during the morning service, that war had been declared against Germany.

12. Permanent Staff

In the 1890s and perhaps long before that, James's foreman was Thomas Seed who lived in the original farm house, where his wife put up the single men. That is all we know about him. About 1904, he was succeeded by young Harry Whittaker, a Lancastrian – but four years later Harry married a girl from his home parish and she did not like Carlton, so they returned to Chipping where she could go back to work, making chairs in a factory. He became self-employed as a colt-breaker for the small farmers of the district. This left him time to travel a Forshaw stallion in the season. In this capacity we shall be able to meet him later.

We turn, therefore, to George Chapman. His father was a carrier at Keelby on the Earl of Yarborough's estate and on leaving school in 1898 George started work in the hunt stables. When he expressed a desire to be with cart horses his lordship, a breeder of them himself and a member of the Shire Horse Society, was kind enough to send him off with a letter to James. The interview was tough. George made up his mind there and then. "I'm not stopping here," he thought – but he did, and stopped there for forty years.

He was eighteen when sent with a horse to the Garstang district of Lancashire, and he travelled that route for the next three seasons. At home, old James once caught him entangled with a girl behind a pub and reprimanded him on the spot.

"We was only having horse play," said George.

"I know what thou wert doing," replied the old man, and told him explicitly. It was about this time his nickname Trunky was bestowed on him by a girl, perhaps the same one. His promotion to foreman at the age of twenty-two was sudden and unexpected.

In stature he was a little chap as all men with big horses should be, and had curly hair which he could lift high off his head with his fingers, and it stayed there, which was a useful party trick. He settled down in due course to a happy marriage with Elizabeth, a local girl, and was always notable for his gentlemanly manners and his kindness, especially to little Mabel Forshaw when her brother Thomas was killed. To keep her mind off that, he fixed her up with little jobs to do. He was popular also with the men in the sense that they liked to play small jokes on him, such as the time in the middle of the night when he had to cross the yard in bitter weather to the lavatory wearing only his nightshirt. One of his lodgers locked him out and so he went into the harness room and wrapped himself in horse blankets. He bore no grudge because it was his own fault. What else would a young man do if someone was careless? He spent the night thinking up his own return trick. A regular practice of underlings was to try the pockets of his coat hanging on a nail. "If you want to know where my cigarettes is," he would always say, "they're in my trousers pocket."

George and Elizabeth had two children, Alec and Doris. Alec joined the staff on leaving school and travelled stallions in various parts of the country until 1939, when Tom got him a job with better prospects in Fremlin's brewery at Maidstone. George's nephew Charlie Butler, who also worked at Carlton as a young man, has described his uncle in words which require no editing.

"He began work before 5.30 and brought his breakfast with him. He went home for his midday meal (12-1) and knocked off at 5. He would come back at 7.30 to feed all the way round. Even his Sunday was as long as an ordinary working day would be now. There was a lot of organising to do. For example, when corn was delivered, someone had to carry it, and that someone would not then be able to exercise a horse. But the exercising had to be kept to time, or the whole day would be buggered up. It was push-and-drive all the time. And then to be responsible for bedding a hundred horses – what a job!"

"A bloody hard worker, he was – and a dedicated one, too. Nothing put him off his job. I remember once he had to put a mare to a three-year-old which had never served one before. It so happened that she was a very big mare, and he was an 'oss with very short legs. This was a problem, and it was made worse by him having such an enormous penis. Uncle had to stoop very low to get a grasp of it and guide it, because the 'oss wasn't clear in his mind what he was trying to do. Things were just about getting sorted out when he took a sudden little step forward and put his foot on George's ankle. He stuck it until the horse had finished. For six months he was on crutches – still doing his job as best he could – and his answer if he was asked why he had been such a bloody fool as to put up with the agony was that the only way to get the 'oss off would have given him a powerful shock. Such a painful experience with his first-ever mare might have put him off his proper work for life. If Mr Tom had been there, and he wasn't, there is no doubt he would have taken the necessary action."

Pidge Hill joined the staff later than Chapman and already had a wife. She lived in Doncaster and he was supposed to pay alimony. The trouble was that he never did. "I'm not paying any bloody maintenance for that bugger," he used to say. The result was that, every now and again, a policeman would arrive and Tom or Jim would come out into the yard and shout for him.

"Hill! HILL!"

"Sir?"

"Go and pack your things. They've come for you again."

Quite cheerfully, or at least more cheerfully than he would have paid maintenance, Hill would go off with the constable, saying "I'll be back in a month, sir".

Off duty he was a smart man and a very good horseman, though he affected to regard the stallion business as a simple matter. If, for example, someone found that a horse was lame, he would say "Don't worry. He can do that job if he can lift his bloody foot over a straw." His colleagues did not know whether he had a baptismal name or even where he had originally come from. If they enquired about the one fact they did know, the existence of his wife, he would answer just as uninformatively. In 1922 he went off to work for someone else. His friends did not even know who that was. He really deserves this prominent

Fig. 30 George Chapman (left) and Fred Wilson with Richard – pictured by *Farmers Weekly* 5th February 1937.

place here only because he had come to the stud earlier than most others – and because he was not the best of influences on George Chapman's bachelor days. In 1939 he reappeared, but was now very unkempt and his habits had fallen far below Carlton standards.

Fred Wilson, the farrier, had been brought up in a little house with a cellar near the Ram Jam Inn at Stretton on the main road between Grantham and Stamford. When he was a boy and his father told him to go down and draw a jug of beer, he was required to whistle continuously in case he drank some himself. This trained him never to become a drinking man. He too came to Carlton not long after George Chapman and was older, having already finished his apprenticeship and acquired a wife. He was even smaller and used to say that a small man had an advantage over a big one, because he could go under the belly of a horse to get to the other side.

His job-interview was rather sticky. Old James was explaining his duties, which would include a number of things in addition to shoeing. It seemed that every time he said, "Well, Wilson, if you come here, you will be doing so-and-so", Wilson would reply with what his wife had told him to say, and begin "Well, sir, my wife says..." At length, James got really exasperated and shouted at him in his broad Lancashire accent, "Look Wilson, I'm hiring thee, not thy wife".

He turned out a good man and Charlie Butler has said of him, "He were but a little chap, yet he could manage all the big 'osses. He only asked a man to help him if one was vicious, to hold him, but lifting the feet, and all that, he did well. And all those new green 'osses he had to deal with! There must have been hundreds shod for their first time by Fred. And any new 'oss that came in, and came to him, he never knew what it would be like, how if would react. He had a striker come in for a couple of hours in the morning, of course – otherwise he did it all himself. He also looked after all the machinery at the stud. His wife put up the single men, you know. With all those lodgers, he used to fetch the coal in, and help his wife."

He sang in the Carlton church choir, and was a very proper man. His most embarrassing experience, at least in public, was with Passmore's mare. Mares that were to be tried were taken one way to the gate and the stallion was supposed to go the other way. It was Fred's lot one day to take Passmore's, and he had to go along the road with her. She was madly on heat. The man with the stallion (and who that was is beyond rediscovery) decided he would break the rule and walk the horse along behind her. Aware that he was there, she stopped. The stallion was halted – against his will, for he was making it as plain as she what they wanted. After a struggle, Fred got her going again, for the time being. Then she would stop once more, and keep on stopping. Fred was fuming because, as the other man had hoped, they seemed to meet all manner of village womenfolk as they continued their flamboyant procession of two. The women were not slow to enjoy the joke.

"What's the matter with your mare, Mr Wilson?"

He ignored this.

"Is she all right? She's behaving funny."

"Shut up."

"Oh, Fred, what's she holding her tail up like that for?"

"SHURRUP," said Fred.

At length they passed from public view, but it was a discomforting morning. All those women! After all, he was a blacksmith, and a good one, not a groom.

On one occasion Chapman, still then a bachelor, and Pidge Hill the pseudo-bachelor, proposed to visit Newark. Fred wanted to come with them. They were reluctant at first but, once he was present, decided to make a real outing of it. Their reasoning was that if Fred was given a night to remember, or one that he could not remember, his wife would certainly see to it that he did not join them again. They got him so drunk that they had a job escorting him back to Newark station for the late train. They then let go of him and discovered he could remain upright, but he was unable to walk forwards. He could go backwards very easily and at speed, but not forwards. So they set him up on the edge of the platform immediately in front of the ladies' waiting-room. Sure enough, Fred started off in reverse with increasing momentum, straight as a die. He crashed the door open, and the cries and shrieks from the ladies within brought the stationmaster along at a trot. He said Fred would have to leave the company's premises, and threatened the other two that they would not be allowed to travel either unless they quietened down. However, after much cajoling, he relented. All three duly boarded the train.

Arriving at Carlton station, Fred showed clear signs of losing the use of his legs entirely, and the only solution was to wheel him in a barrow. They took him most of the way, and debated what was to be done next. Neither relished the thought of conveying him right home to his cottage and to Mrs Wilson. So they decided to leave him where he was. The remarkable thing was that, as he disclosed later, he could very clearly hear every single word of what was said, and the conversation much depressed him, but he could neither see nor speak. Nor, of course, could he get out of the barrow.

At five o'clock next morning, he was still there. But the cool air had done much for his physical powers and the sound of voices not only woke him but restored to him the gift of forward motion. Early arrivals for work were astounded to see him progressing earnestly, if not gracefully, in the direction of his cottage. The greeting he received inside it was never divulged.

Although he claimed never to have made a penny from putting up the single men, Fred eventually saved enough to buy the house he lived in, and another behind it as well. He had a son who married and kept a shop in Sheffield, selling tobacco, sweets and ice cream. He himself always swore that he would never work for anyone but the Forshaws, and never did.

The Ashpoles begin, for us at least, with the father, Alf, who lived at Bedford and travelled Forshaw stallions regularly from some date in the 1890s, nearly always for the Bedford Shire Horse Society. His wife had an annual baby and Tom, visiting him every year, used to say "Well, Ashpole, what is it this time?" The answer was usually "Girl, sir," for only five of the fourteen were boys. Two of these, Jim and the youngest, another Alf who was born in 1899, worked for Carlton whole-time, while the other three were seasonal leaders like their father.

Jim arrived in 1904. He once went to Argentina with a consignment of stallions to Señor Casares. Another time he went to Russia with horses. That was in 1914 and war broke out while he was away. He had an awful job to get back. He managed it in the end, joined the Coldstream Guards and after 18 months was shot in the arm and invalided out at Aberdeen in 1917. He came back to Carlton and married one of the girls who had nursed him.

He once spotted Bill Hardy (then a whole-time bachelor, who will appear later as a seasonal man) creeping off somewhere on a Sunday morning and later found him asleep on some hay. So he got the others to queue up and urinate in his ear. Bill woke up and said,

"What are you doing that for?"

Jim explained,

"If you find a weasel asleep, you always want to piss in its ear."

He often went out as a leader and had Bradgate Premier for its first six seasons as a Carlton horse, and then switched to a stallion called Donation, which he claimed was the only one regularly mentioned on the wireless – in the Appeal on Sunday evenings, always ending up by telling people where to send their donation. Unlike his prolific parents, the Jim Ashpoles never managed to produce even one child.

Alf the younger joined the staff in the mid-1920s. His trouble was the drink. He once went on a roundabout at a fair in Bedford and thoughtlessly sat on one of the outside horses. He fell off and crashed to the ground. He found that he could get about quite well with the aid of a broom held upside down, but he was not much use at the stud until he was better. His colleagues told him that, just because he could manage Shire stallions, he was daft to think he could ride the golden gallopers. His only answer was that it was the way they went up and down on them poles that flummoxed him.

He travelled at times, though not so often as his brother. Towards the end of a day his horse could easily hold him up as they went along, but he did admit that on one occasion he was compelled to have a little sleep on a wide verge at the road side. When he woke up, he found that the stallion was still there, grazing around him. On passing the same spot a week later, he was amazed to find a patch of long grass, the size and shape of his own body, surrounded by short grass with a pile of drying horse dung near the outline of his head.

He was a very competent man, like all Ashpoles, and very obliging. When Tom was expecting some visitors early on a Monday morning to see stallions, he asked him, "Would you mind cleaning out these four on a Sunday?"

"Yes, I'll do that, Mr Forshaw, with pleasure."

When Tom got back from church, he could not see Alf anywhere, but at last found him in the office with a horse.

"Whatever are you in here for?"

Fig. 31 After demobilisation Tom Curtis was undecided whether to join the Police or come to Carlton.

"Well, Mr Forshaw, I thought it would be warmer for him in here."

He had married an ex-land girl who was an extremely good milker. She always wore a spotless white coat, and Jim Forshaw admired her for that. He said she really *looked* like a dairy maid. The eldest child, when he was fourteen, went off and got a job in Bedford.

Tom Curtis from Hucknall was a very young trooper in the South Notts Hussars in the second half of the war and was one of six soldiers allotted on temporary release to Carlton in the 1918 season. He had a Forshaw pedigree, his father having worked whole-time for James in the distant past – indeed, he had the distinction of being the very first man to stable a stallion in the new boxes at Carlton when the general move from Blyth took place thirty years before. On demobilisation he started work at £6 a month and board, decided against staying, went home, thought he would join the Police and was persuaded by Tom to change his mind.

One Sunday evening in church a girl took his eye and he managed to speak to her afterwards. She raised no objection when he offered to escort her to Carlton Hall, where she was a servant, but when she learned where he worked she left him as fast as her legs could carry her, and he never saw her again. However, not long after, he married Elsie Taylor, the daughter of his landlady who at times had up to seventeen of the single men staying with her. When Tom Forshaw learned the honeymoon was to be at Southsea, he offered the bride and groom a free ride in a horse box for part of the way, the horse to be handed over to someone at King's Cross. That was a bit of a saving.

From 1920 he regularly travelled a stallion for the Saffron Walden Society. His own account of one or two occurrences fortunately survives. On the return journey at the end of the very first season, when two horses were hired, he and Cherry Downes, the other groom, were sitting in the small compartment at the end of the box. "We smelt burning, and as we were on the back of an express with no communication cord, we were in a right mess, especially with the horses getting restive. Luckily a signalman spotted the fire, and we were shunted off before any real damage was done. Another time again behind a main-line express, the undercarriage and wheels of the box were pulled clean off, leaving me and a horse sitting on the line in the box. They stopped all traffic, and we got rescued."

When walking his route, "I had permission to go across a park, which saved me miles of walking. One week when I arrived, the estate had put up a six foot post and rail fence, right across my way, and while I was moaning to myself about the long walk back, the horse which weighed over a ton suddenly leapt the fence without touching a rail and left me holding the leading rein on the wrong side. When I got to the village they wanted to know how I had got across the park. I told them me and the horse just hopped over the fence, but before they would believe me, I think the whole village went to look at the footings. This same horse always used to play up when passing a certain spot in the wood, and I used to wonder the reason, until someone discovered there had been a dead man hanging from a tree for about three weeks."

At the stud, "some of the thirty-odd paddocks joined the Carlton estate woods, and at shooting times we used to hide behind the tumbrils, and collect the birds which dropped in the paddocks. The shooters and beaters and dogs dare not come and retrieve them, cause the stallions would go for them open-mouthed. When I used to see Faulkner the keeper, and ask him if they had had a good day, he was not very polite, but there was a good smell in the kitchen at home."

Tom's reliability, good sense and able horsemanship were an enormous asset to the Forshaw family and he fully deserved his position as No 2 to George Chapman. He was also a good showman, though he rarely had an opportunity to shine in that way. Someone offered him a job at twice what he earned at

Fig. 32 When Tom Curtis was asked to show a stallion, he always did it well.

Carlton, but he turned it down. He said he would never leave, for three times as much.

Cherry Downes, his colleague on the Saffron Walden route in 1920, stood 6' 3" and was an immensely powerful man with arms of simian length and huge hands. The Forshaw brothers no doubt knew what the initial A of his first name represented, but no one else did. He was simply Cherry on account of his nose, which contrasted sharply with the rest of his features. He had been a Carlton man since just before the war, had travelled Saffron Walden the previous year, was a very competent horseman and was about twice as old as Curtis, but these were his only qualifications as mentor to the less experienced man. Working their separate routes during the week, they lodged at the same place at the weekend.

One Saturday afternoon, two girls were looking over a wall at the stallions and Cherry came across to them and invited them to the pictures in the evening. At the tryst, Tom found that his girl was a dwarf: behind that wall, she had been standing on a barrel. He gallantly bought two tickets and took her in, but as soon as they came out he made a quick getaway. At the end of the season, the last Sunday dinner was the best they had had, for Cherry had presented their landlady with a duck he had stolen from one place, plenty of peas picked from another and some new potatoes from her own garden. These he had grubbed up with his fingers and then stuck the haulms into the soil again.

A bellicose man, Cherry would steal anything, but he was never caught red-handed. When two years later his newest hobby was fishing for Forshaw hens with a net operated on a pole from behind a hedge, Richard, fresh from school and keen, proposed to lay in wait for him. His father, who had no desire to have his son's head knocked off his young shoulders, forbade it. So Cherry, as good with cattle as with horses, did not get the sack until 1926. After he had left to go to another good job, it came to the Forshaw ears that, in the hope that the General Strike would lead to a successful people's revolution, he had organised the distribution of all the stallions among the staff. Ownership of

Lincoln What's Wanted II, the new London champion, was to be vested in himself.

Joe Gaskin, who eventually weighed just over 18 stones and had red hair, took out his first Carlton stallion in 1917. In 1920 he joined the full-time staff and Richard in his schooldays often used to come across his uncle, who was employed as a bricklayer at Repton. For sixteen years Joe was sent out to a variety of counties ranging from Cheshire to Hampshire with stallions let to the Mobberley, Kingston-on-Soar, Cambridgeshire and Isle of Ely, Nottingham, Welback Tenants (Duke of Portland) and Fareham Societies. He saved up a lot of money and in 1932 got a small holding of his own and left. Unfortunately, his venture was a disaster, for could not make a go of it and his wife died. He came back in 1937 and married a new one, Daisy, who had two illegitimate children.

He now had an even bigger belly than when he had left. Tom Forshaw told him he could probably get rid of some of it if he started work half an hour earlier than the others and finished half an hour later, but he was quite comfortable as he was. He wore enormous trousers that were very slack in front – as he said, he liked to have plenty of ballroom. He was not, however, by any means a flabby man. He was very powerful and, in spite of his awkward size and shape, an expert milker. He is said to have won a £50 prize offered by the Bath and West Agricultural Society for anyone who could milk a cow faster than the new Alpha-Laval machine they had on view. The only time his trousers were to cause him any difficulty was when a cow called Carlton Penelope kicked and got a hind leg down inside them. She could not fathom her error and tried to stand on it. Joe had resumed stallion-leading on his return, but if he was required to show a horse to potential customers at home he did it very badly.

Arthur Mumford, a local man, was an army corporal in the war and joined the firm after it. He was an extremely conscientious and sensible person and was usually put in charge if Chapman and Curtis were both away, as they were during the London Shows. Mabel Forshaw asked to go to the Show when she was thirteen, but her father said she was too young. To compensate, he did send her two telegrams in the course of it. The first listed the Carlton prizes won on the Tuesday – three firsts, a second, third and fifth. Very importantly, she took it to Mumford, who pinned it on the board. When the second one, next day, announced that Lincoln What's Wanted II had won the championship the ritual was repeated with even grander ceremony. Mumford married Joe Gaskin's stepdaughter and sometimes fought with him – they would both appear, the next morning, with black eyes.

Before we proceed to a selected few of the minor players on the Carlton scene, Chapman's nephew Charlie Butler deserves a longer notice, disproportionate to his length of service. He represents for us those Forshaw-trained men who were instrumental in the success of other well-known enterprises and also provides a good example of the pleasure Tom took in seeing a promising young fellow get on in life.

Charlie was fifteen, as young as the twentieth century, when he first reported for work and was sent to join four others as lodger with Mrs Wilson. He helped

Fig. 33 Hawton Blend at the Stud Farm, with Arthur Mumford.

to feed the horses in the fields at 5.30, and then helped to muck out the stables. Counting young stock and geldings collected for their Army call-up, about 130 horses had to be got ready for the day. After two hours' hard work, the breakfast half hour was something for a growing boy to look forward to – and, as the war progressed, an increasing disappointment. What a tiny piece of bacon! He asked Mrs Wilson if he could have all the week's ration in one day. She did her best for him, poor dear, but it was his uncle who kept him alive. George always seemed to have a bit of his midday bait left over and it was only many years later that Charlie realised how far his Aunt Lizzie must have sacrificed herself for him by putting a bit extra in her husband's box.

He had his head well screwed on and realised that, with more and more men being taken for the war, he would have opportunities that he might have to wait years for in normal times. So he did everything he was told as well as he could, and did not worry that his twelve-and-six a week worked out at about twopence an hour. When winter came, he exercised eight stallions a day, and calculated the walking distance of this part of his job as 26 miles. Going up and down that lane, he never tried to stop for a quick adolescent smoke, because he knew it was out of the question to avoid being spotted.

His sixteenth birthday brought a chance to tackle a job on his own. The valuable Tandridge Coming King, let to the Oswestry Society, had caught a venereal disease from one of the mares and he was sent off post-haste with Leonardo II as substitute. "This," he remembered as long as he lived, "was a real bugger of a horse." He handed him over to the groom, Fred Taylor, and stayed on to treat the pox. He found it no easy job, for he had to tie Coming

King up near a mare to get his penis erected and then sponge it with the medicine provided for him. After a fortnight's dedicated effort he had the horse fit to resume duty and brought the real bugger of a substitute home again.

The following year, now a well-built and powerful young man, he had his first experience of travelling. An old celebrity Drayman XXIII was now eighteen, a year older than himself, and his career in high society had finished. But Tom had let him, for a final season, to a certain lady who kept four stallions, each of a different breed, at Bedfont on premises occupying what is now the southern end of Heathrow airport. Charlie was worried when he heard that his temporary boss was to be a woman and alarmed when she began by asking him to show a Thoroughbred stallion at Kingston market. "I didn't know one end of a Thoroughbred from another." However, that was safely accomplished, and he began to travel the immense and venerable Drayman.

There were not many mares for him, which was of course why the Forshaws had allowed him to go. All went smoothly for some time, except for the excruciating half-hour interview at the end of each week with the shrewd Mrs X. He had to describe in detail all the week's activities and answer a series of penetrating questions. "I used to blush so often during the Saturday half-hour that I longed to get out of the room." When he grew to man's estate, he began to realise that this terrible woman had been secretly amused by his bashfulness and enjoyed forcing him to say things that he had been brought up to believe were taboo in drawing-rooms.

One morning, having served a mare, old Drayman was proceeding along the road at Windsor, not far from the Castle, when he fell. There he lay and Charlie scratched his head. "I had a bloody hard job to get him up, too," but get him up he did, and gently ushered the old warrior home. Another horse was sent to complete the season, but after it was all over, Drayman died.

The next year, he travelled Walburg King in Worcestershire, on an incredibly long route. On a Thursday, he had to do 26 miles, excluding any detours to farms. In 1919, he remained at Carlton and the following season took Walburg King back to Worcestershire. He had a marvellous time in 1921, travelling the four-year-old Carlton Friar Tuck for the Louth society. They were hiring two Carlton stallions this year. For this one they had paid £1,000 and were charging twelve guineas a service. But he was a remarkable horse. He 'stopped' most of his mares the first time and so many men wanted to use him that, on Charlie's assurance that he was in good form, Tom gave the society permission for 30 extra ones. At the end of the season, computing his wages, his groom's fees and his bonus for bringing his charge home in good condition, Charlie felt he was something of a Rockefeller. During the season he had lived entirely on half-crowns.

His dealings in 1922 and 1923 were with the most famous stallion in England, the redoubtable Rickford Coming King. This horse requires his own mini-biography in a later chapter, where these two years in Charlie's life are more conveniently considered. Before going off on his holidays after the second season, he asked Jim whether it would matter if he was away a bit longer,

Fig. 34 Forshaw-trained with stallions from the age of 15 until he was 23, Charlie Butler spent the rest of his working life at Young's Brewery, Wandsworth, where he had the opportunity to become the outstanding gelding man of his time.

because his father was unwell. As always at this slack time, permission was granted more than willingly. It saved the firm money.

At the London Show earlier in the year, 'commercial' gelding classes for single horses, pairs and teams yoked to vehicles had been introduced for the first time and Mann, Crossman and Paulin of the Albion Brewery in the Whitechapel Road had won all three classes as well as taking two second prizes. This stung Young's Brewery in Wandsworth to join battle and during Charlie's leave of absence they enquired for a man to set them up in the show business. Tom knew that Charlie wanted to marry (he was now 23) and they had no suitable accommodation. Jim wrote to him. "Do you want a job in London?" So Charlie never went back to Carlton after his holiday. He was followed to Young's by a brown four-year-old gelding which they named Bob.

John Roberts, labourer, was a cord-round-the-corduroys sort of man and always easy game for jokers, as when he found his dinner-box contained only a dead rabbit. One day some boys let his cockerel out, his pride and joy. "Mr Roberts, your cockerel's out." Out of the cottage he came, to get him in again. All the boys helped, taking care, every time he looked like catching him, to drive him a bit farther off. At length, John lost his temper. He got his gun and shot it. "That'll teach the bugger a lesson," he said. His wife railed at him bitterly for this, so he said, "and I'll make your bloody bones rattle too" and that shut her up.

Being a regular chapel man, John did not swear on Sundays unless unduly provoked. George Chapman would sometimes meet him on the way home from worship and walk along with him, bumping into him every now and again until John would exclaim, "What do you bloody think you're doing, you daft bugger?" George himself attended either church or chapel impartially, but only at harvest festival.

Other men, and regrettably only a few, must here be confined to a small space. Fritz and Wilhelm (were these really their names or only tokens?) as prisoners of war taken in 1917, were then of course literally confined, except when working in the fields, as they had been accustomed to do before the war when free. Jim told his little niece Mabel to keep away from them – "they could be dangerous": but her mother thought they were very sad and gave them a little extra food because she was sorry for them.

There were, inevitably, other unfortunates. None of the men could communicate with the deaf-mute any better than they had been able to do with prisoners. His identity was confined within himself. Except for Jim who paid his wages and Tom who went to the trouble of learning the sign-language in order to tell him what to do, no one knew where he had come from nor whither he eventually went and even his name is now lost. Poor Hugh Midwinter broke his pelvis when a young stallion he was attempting to load into a box at the dock on the railway siding suddenly reared up. He had to be replaced, and Jim could not or would not reinstate him when he was fit. Sam Chamberlain was made redundant in 1927 in an economy drive and all he could expect in those days was a good reference.

There had always been a number of Lancastrians at Carlton. Percy Greenwood, son of a small farmer, had come at the end of the war. Though an able and reliable man, he was often bad-tempered with the stallions and when in 1930 he had the chance to take a small farm in his own county, the Forshaws wished him good luck and did not grieve to see him go. John Porter had a similar background and is best remembered for his strict view on morality. When Tom brought some visitors round one day and said "Here's a gentleman you'll know, John – this is Mr Y and his wife come to see us". When they had gone, John indignantly told his boss, "That weren't his bloody wife. And he knew I knew it weren't his bloody wife." John eventually left to work for the Princess Royal. William Graham, also from Lancashire, was intermittently rather than regularly whole-time. He would do anything, go anywhere, replace anyone off sick and always came at harvest to stook sheaves, at which he excelled. He sometimes also led a stallion – for Mobberley, Wetherby or Welbeck or on the Isle of Man.

Johnny Jones from Anglesey was very short and the other men recommended that when he went out with his girl friend he ought to take a bucket, either to stand on or to put over her head and use the handle to pull himself up. He was a good chap, an excellent groom and enchanted Sutton churchgoers with his beautiful voice. He never travelled, being kept for duty at home in the season. He left too soon for the good of Carlton and got his first farm, married and had his first child all in the same week. Ernest Vaux came as a young fellow in 1936 from his father's small farm in Yorkshire. Tom and Jim were glad when he started courting a Sutton girl and married her, for they always liked to see their men settle down unless they were destined for higher things.

Bert Spencer from Willingham in Cambridgeshire was noted for his pencil and notebook. He wrote important things down, especially memoranda of overtime, but never when he slipped off early. When free he played cricket, though lethargically. The Carlton ground had no marked boundaries because of the long grass and trees and in one Married v Single match he watched a fellow-fielder frantically searching for the ball. As the panting batsmen were completing their fifth run Bert came to his aid and said, "If you want the ball, it's under the fifth nettle on your right".

Tiddly Martin came in the early Thirties. War service had given him not only a military air but sciatica. He was frequently off work until Richard persuaded him to wear long-johns – but those did not cure him of being often late in the mornings. When he was unable to walk at night, the landlord of the Lord Nelson in Sutton always drove him home to safety. He was noted for possessing a dog called The Bugger, which he led on an unnecessarily and inconveniently long piece of string. Just before the second war, he left to take a job in the brewery at Newark.

Cuzzy Wood had farmed at Southwell until everything went wrong for him, including the loss of his wife who ran off perhaps because they were incompatible. She was very refined and he was a bucolic type – tall, bandy-legged and always wearing a flat cap, grandad shirt, riding breeches held up by braces and an enormous belt, and huge brown boots encrusted with dung. He came to Carlton in 1939 and lodged with Tom and Elsie Curtis. An easy-going type, he had one fixed rule. "Never let this week's wages get mixed up with the next," he used to say. So he always spent everything by Saturday evening, when he was paid. If he miscalculated, he would borrow ten shillings from Curtis and pay it back before Sunday. Elsie once offered to cut his hair and he was startled when he found she had dyed it bright green.

13. The Annual Round

The end of the Carlton year is easier to identify than its beginning. By early July, the covering season was over and the horses let their tail-hair down for a long outdoor holiday at home, free of all routine. The regular staff, back at full strength, now had a much reduced workload and could take their own holidays. Paid ones lasted a bare week even at the end of the Thirties, but if a man asked for six weeks' leave of absence he was more than welcome to have it.

Only the major agricultural shows, and for obvious reasons only the minority which took place in late summer, had stallion classes. These were something of a nuisance, but it was often necessary to exhibit in order to keep the firm's name before the eye of a wider public than the few thousands who visited Islington in February. Horses on this duty had their vacation delayed or interrupted, and a few were destined never to have one. For one reason or another they had come to the end of their useful careers. Even if the only failing was a lack or loss of fertility, the Forshaws would never castrate a mature horse. So, on what Tom called "hanging day", they were sent off to Aubrey Hughes for slaughter. No one enjoyed loading up the condemned at the siding and men would weep to see an old favourite go. But pride ensured that even on their last twelve-mile journey horses never left the stud unless well groomed, plaited and smart.

The only memorable mishap during the holiday period occurred one year towards the end of it. The hunt, in spite of several boards placed at intervals and in large letters bearing the message KEEP OUT, found itself in the 16-acre field with a collection of stallions and colts. Most of the riders were still coming in when the leaders were already doing their best to get out again. Pandemonium reigned. The stallions' natural instinct for battle against interlopers was immediately aroused but they also abandoned the tacit solidarity that had been achieved by their temporary bachelorhood when they realised that there were mares present. Ladies dismounted and ran for the gate. Gentlemen tried to show their gallantry. Carlton staff arrived in force. Eventually everyone got out and the stallions were kept in with surprisingly little damage done. The next time they hunted in that part of the country, the Master said, "We're going down Carlton way. So for God's sake keep out of Forshaws' bloody birdcage."

Though Tom was always on the lookout for any young animals whose potential no one had spotted, most recruits joined the equine staff in the autumn as foals, after weaning. They had either taken the eye at a foal show or had been recommended earlier by acute leaders in the course of their travels. If in any one year eight stallions had departed on hanging day, twelve foals were purchased, provided that their parentage supported their claim to notice.

When assembled, these babies were sent to J H Dennick, a farmer and corn merchant of King's Lynn, whose land was ideal for rearing young stock. Richard usually escorted them on the train. Since Mr Dennick's scruples prevented him having anything that he did not own, on the place, he bought them, paying cash. Richard then paid their keep for the next six months, bought back last year's foals and settled up for their board and lodging during the final half-year. If one were to have died while in his care, Dennick would have been the loser in law, but he never failed at some time during the visit to quote Romans 12.10: "Be kindly affectioned one to another in brotherly love, in honour preferring one another". His extremely tall son, who was always present, never said anything much but no doubt subscribed to St Paul's sentiment, as did Richard. So the law would never come into it.

When Richard came home with last year's foals, they had to be assessed. A few were obvious candidates for the stud book and the necessary forms were duly dispatched to 12 Hanover Square. A decision about the others could be delayed until the spring, when they were two years old. Those which had failed to develop satisfactorily were then castrated and sold.

In naming horses the registered and exclusive prefix 'Carlton' could be used. This system had been inaugurated in 1893 in order to prevent the confusion caused by two or more horses having the same name (otherwise only soluble by quoting their five-digit stud book numbers, a most clumsy procedure) and also to enable people easily to identify an animal with a particular stud. James had been one of the first 105 members of the Shire Horse Society to apply for this privilege, but only occasionally used it and his sons followed him in this. If all their stallions' names began with the same word, the sheer number of them would obscure rather than clarify their identities. It was better to devise a unique and inventive name – without of course reaching the fanciful heights, or depths, that mark the naming of race horses.

When winter routine resumed at the stud, it was Chapman, Jimmy Ashpole, Curtis and Mumford who began the day by giving the horses the small 5.30 feed of chopped hay and oat straw, bran and oats. At 6 o'clock, mucking out started. The horses were bedded on sawdust. This was brought in by rail to the siding and was stored as a mini-mountain in the centre of the covered yard. In contrast to old James's practice, no peat moss was used. By 7.30 all was finished and the horses had been given a full feed. Breakfast time for the staff was 7.30 till 8 but Richard took till 8.30 because he breakfasted at home.

Grooms had then to examine all horses to check for any troubles, paying special attention to legs and feet, watching for incipient grease and reporting anything amiss to Chapman. During this time, he was in charge of chopping hay and straw. "It's a wonder they never got farmer's lung," Richard reflected in later years, "shaking up hay which was often so dusty you could hardly see." For that reason an extractor fan was installed in the early Thirties. Wilson ground the oats, which were all purchased, or more often, received from someone who owed money for service – a mutually acceptable method of payment, especially on the struggling farmer's side during these hard years. Bran was all bought from the miller. One former employee said, "When it came to mixing the feed, the Forshaws took it in turns to see it done, one in the mornings, another in the evenings, and swapping over the next week. Measured to the last ounce, it was, and every horse studied. They all had different appetites, you see, and different wants. 'Osses aren't bloody machines."

Fred Croft, as universally respected among Shire people as any man ever was, had never been a Carlton man, but knew what he was talking about when he said, "Everything there was done by the Forshaws themselves – everything that mattered anyway. By which I mean they either did do it, or else told someone exactly what to do – whether it was to put a horse in no. 1 box or no. 10 or no. 23, as the case may be, or whether it was something else. There was little scope there for a man to use his initiative – though if a man had any, and wanted to use it, there was no better place to learn and no bosses more likely to give a promising young fellow a helping hand to better himself somewhere else."

Exercising the horses in full stallion harness occupied most of the winter day. Each man would do three miles with each horse he took out – to the end of the lane and back again and always in view of the house, as planned in the Eighties by old James. All the way, the groom had to hold his hand at the level of the horse's mouth. If a horse did not hold his head up properly, a "dumb jockey" (bearing rein) was used. "If he learns to hold his head up, he'll soon pick up his feet," Tom used to say. Each groom would exercise up to eight horses. This drudgery was broken by the dinner hour from 12 o'clock, when the horses also had a feed. In very bad weather, six stallions could be exercised simultaneously round the perimeter of the indoor ring. The sawdust hill in the middle meant that each was following the one in front of him and could not try to dash across and attack another. If a groom thought in the morning that this indoor walk was a refreshing change from going down the lane and back, he would have changed his mind by the end of it. The last feed was at 5, but the men knocked off only when they finished the day's work. Hay was put in to occupy the horses' minds when Chapman made his last round at night.

Saturday was a full day, like the first five. On the day of rest, there was no exercising and, after the Twenties, the men were allowed alternate Sundays off. Those on duty came in at the usual time, but knocked off at nine. They returned at four to feed and then went home to enjoy the remainder of the weekend uninterrupted, except for Chapman.

Since stallion licences were valid only for one year and had to be returned to the Ministry before the end of October, it was necessary as soon as possible after that to apply or reapply on behalf of all entire horses which would be two years old or more in the following year. In the Thirties the number of Carlton stallions holding licences, though fluctuating, increased slightly – 64 in 1930 followed by 65, 61, 69, 71, 68, 70, 79, 77 and in 1939, 72. The Ministry vet spent two whole days examining the candidates. He was extremely conscientious, perhaps hoping to find a failure. He never did and it would be amazing if he had ever been given a chance to do so. He always claimed that it would take him another two days at home to write up all the reports. He believed that it would demonstrate to his superiors his meticulous attention to detail and duty if he put something of a mildly critical nature in the 'Comments' column,

Fig. 35 One of Gilbert Parsons' earliest pictures, tricking us into assuming that Present King II, London champion in 1906, is posing for the camera unaided. An unrecognisable man, shadows and distant trees on a surviving original print have been turned to grass and sky by retouching.

even if the sheet related to the finest stallion. So, to save embarrassment all round, he would get Richard to write down all the names and add his own observations – such as "Goes wide behind", "Rather long-backed", "A trifle twisted in front", "A little short of foot", and so on. Richard believed he was the only stallion-man in England who volunteered derogatory remarks about his own animals. But it did no harm, and made the vet most grateful and thank-you-very-much Mr Forshaw. During these visitations, except for the hullo-how-are-you and a goodbye, Tom got on with his own work, but it was very different when Parsons came.

G H Parsons, from Alsager, was the photographer. *The* photographer. There was none to touch him for portraits of heavy horses. Not to have your stallions or prizewinning mares photographed by Parsons was a sign that you were second-class. He was a perfectionist. He would spend an hour, if need be, just to get one horse standing right, with his head right and his ears right and his expression alert and intelligent. It is certain that no photographer since his day has matched G H Parsons. Few could match him for swearing, either. He was a smallish man, very untidy, with pockets full of holes burnt by his pipe. While his pipe was cooling, he smoked cigarettes. Even though the older stallions would not need re-photographing for the route cards, he always stayed a night with Tom and Bessie at the Stud House. An ashtray was prominently placed in his room and there was evidence that he used it, but there were never any fag-ends. Bessie at length discovered that he threw them up on top of the wardrobe.

On arrival he asked only for two assistants – a groom to hold the horse and Richard – but it never worked out like that. Tom would have to be there and, just as the horse was pretty well right, would interfere, perhaps by waving a handkerchief to attract its interest and make it prick its ears. Then, as likely as not, it would also move a leg.

"Get out of the bloody way," Parsons once roared, losing his patience completely. "I can get on better without you."

There was a moment of silent awe. As soon as that particular horse had been done at last, the groom spread the news like wildfire. "Here, d'you know what Parsons told the Old Man? Told him to get out of the bloody way!"

The clever thing about Parsons was that he was just as handy with a brush. It was child's play for him to paint the groom out of the picture and replace him with a completed brick wall background or grass and sky. He could just as easily remove an offending penis which emerged at an inconvenient moment from its sheath, even if it became erect: if this happened, the horse would be standing up well, with a lively look on its face. Parsons was a marvel at painting grass. He usually asked Tom's opinion of a horse, in case there were any little blemishes that needed putting right in the photograph.

The Shire Horse Show, which began always on the Tuesday of the last week in February, was reduced from four days to only three in 1926, when there were 325 horses present, excluding the fifty entries and more than fifty horses in the 'commercial' classes. Though this number was only 38% of the 1904 record, there was no fall in standard, for only the very best were now competing and these had benefited from nearly half a century of the stud book movement, to a degree that only those who, like Tom, had attended the first few Shows were in a position to appreciate.

At Carlton, preparations were begun six months ahead, when the 'London horses' were selected – not necessarily the best six, because if it was considered that any were unlikely to stand higher than they had before, they were not included. "If you get to the top, the only way forward is downward," Tom used to say. Like the University Boat Race, the London Show required half a year's training for just a few minutes' trial, with no intermediate rounds or encounters. Men on the Thames and horses at Islington had to reach the peak of perfection on exactly the right day; and from peaks, if reached too soon, there was only decline.

As the time drew near, Richard himself took over the exercising of these stallions whenever he had time, and if he did all six in a day that took most of it. Tom also used to go into training. It requires good horsemanship to make a stallion stand still and proudly 'on his legs', as if posing for Parsons, not only while the judge is examining him but as long as he is in the ring (Those who lounge about or talk to others, as some do today, when the judge is busy elsewhere, would have horrified him). It takes skill to walk him away, turn and walk back again in a dead straight line as the judge watches how his hind legs and then his front ones go. To repeat the performance at the trot demands an ability to move efficiently in step with the horse. The handler has to take

Fig. 36 A press photographer's shot of Coleshill Field Marshal, winner of the gold medal in the Norfolk Spring Stallion Show at Norwich, 1939. The caption-writer assumed the handler was "Mr T Forshaw." In fact it was Mr J Forshaw.

abnormally long strides and lift his knees in an exaggerated manner. The right hand must be held high to the horse's mouth, the left arm kept motionless and the trunk and head (with a hat on top) always vertical as if running smoothly on rails rather than propelled by the two pistons below. While the horse's powerful and free-flowing movement inspires awe in the spectator and, if all his legs move straight and true, approval in the eyes of the judge, the gait of the man is essentially grotesque and ridiculous. Tom aimed, from a standing start, to set off without a preliminary shuffle, as if he and the horse were responding to a conductor's baton. He always did the same number of paces with every horse on each outward and return journey. The halfway turn was executed uniformly on each occasion. Possibly the last of the moderns whose standard in this performance equalled that of Tom Forshaw and the best of his contemporaries was the late Reg Nunn, who once worked at Carlton between one head man's job and another.

As he grew older, Tom was afraid of cramp seizing his legs at the trot and practised regularly not only with the show horses, but sometimes without one. A chance and ignorant caller at the house, seeing him on the lawn trotting solo as if holding an invisible horse, would have concluded that he had witnessed the ultimate in behavioural disorder. In 1926, however, he had passed his sixtieth birthday and resigned himself to handing over the showing by stages to Richard, who from 1930 exhibited them all. He was as good as his uncle and equally impeccable in his dress and personal appearance. Tom continued, with the help of his youngest daughter Mabel, to spend winter evenings cutting the ribbons, blue and white in the firm's colours, and wired them all himself.

Early on the Monday morning of Show week, Chapman and four others left with the horses in boxes hitched to a passenger train, with the Carlton station-master on behalf of the Company ceremoniously waving them off and wishing them good luck. On arrival at King's Cross, the horses were walked to the Hall. It was not much more than a mile and they could have gone up the Pentonville Road, but the police made them use little side roads – keeping to the left, whereas they were accustomed to face oncoming vehicles. This, and the noise of the traffic, was liable to upset them and they frequently had to be blindfolded. Bessie's enormous hamper and special box full of home-made meat pies, bacon, bread, eggs, cakes and all manner of other delicacies travelled with them on the train, but were delivered together with all the other paraphernalia to the Hall by the railway company. Chapman always used to say that the food was what made him look forward to the Show. Richard sometimes travelled by a later train with his uncle and father and the rest of the family, but more often than not accompanied the horses to assist their passage through the streets and even lead one himself. Either Curtis or Mumford would be left in charge at home.

Preparations for the breeding season followed close upon the heels of the Show and before the beginning of April routine had given way to a situation where no day was quite like any other. The majority of the stallions went off to their seasonal headquarters: so too, as we have seen, did some of the regular men – this is not to say that they were out of sight and mind for the next thirteen weeks. Whenever a horse was unable to continue his duties, for whatever reason and even if for only a few days, a substitute had to be sent. The firm prided itself on the speed with which this could be done. To take one example, a telephone call was received one evening to say that a three-year-old, one of five stallions let to the Rydedale society, was suffering from laminitis, and a substitute would be needed. Richard had a few hours' sleep, then got up in the middle of the night and drove to Helmsley, arriving at six in the morning. He found that it was not fever in the feet at all, but chest founder to which a young horse, still somewhat narrow between the forelegs, might be subject if called upon to serve a succession of wide-backed mares. The horse could not carry on, and he immediately telephoned the Stud House. A substitute was put on the train at seven and arrived before noon.

Tom worked on the basis of having one substitute available for every three or four horses sent out on rounds. This also enabled what might be called 'tactical' substitutions to be made – replacing a horse which was not getting on very well or not as popular as expected, or relieving or assisting one which was being overdone. In the later Thirties, a motor box was occasionally used if this would be quicker, but in general and for all long distances rail was more efficient, speedy and economical. James's old system still operated, whereby tickets could be made out at Carlton for any railway journey by horse or man, including the family or anyone else. As soon as the deposited float had been used up, the company would notify Richard who would write a cheque for £50 to top it up. As for enquiring how to travel from anywhere in England to any-where else, the thing to do was to ask Tom who, as his father had been, was not only a walking stud book but a living Bradshaw. He always knew the best route.

The grooms were remarkably fit and rarely had to be substituted themselves. However, the Brigg secretary did once telephone to say theirs had disappeared. Richard, who took the call, was informed that the horse was still in his box. "We're not going in there with that bugger, and we're not going to get him out, either. He'll bloody well kill someone. We've shoved some feed over the door at him and got some water in, in a bucket – but that's all he'll get." It is not surprising that the horse was in an emotional state. One of the permanent staff was dispatched post-haste but soon after he arrived the original leader reappeared, explaining that he had gone off with some woman and it had taken a day and a half to get what he called "the fussy" completed.

At home in the season, mares were coming and going all the time. Some were walked over from farms up to a dozen miles away, served by a stallion (usually one of the cheaper ones) and taken home again. A proportion of these had to be brought back again three weeks later when a new oestrus showed that they had not held to the first service. Others came by rail and stayed six weeks in order to make as certain as possible that they had conceived. These had been booked to one of the expensive horses retained at home to make them available to anyone in England or Wales who particularly wanted to use them. This monstrous regiment of mares was so large that, as soon as one of them came off the train, Chapman entered her name and particulars of her colour and markings against her owner's name in a book and Wilson simultaneously branded her on top of her near fore foot with the number corresponding to that in the book. Without such a system one boggles at the succession of errors that would be instituted by even one look-alike being returned perhaps to Cornwall in error instead of to Hull.

The Forshaws were proud of the attention these boarders received. Sam Littler the vet came twice a week, as his father had done before him and, although this was really unnecessary, it was a wise precaution against the sort of men who, on principle, would find something to complain about in the hope of getting the fee and charge for keep reduced. He provided a separate bill for each mare examined. Jim paid up promptly (a rare experience for any veterinary surgeon) and entered the appropriate figure on each owner's account (Owners rarely paid him promptly). Not uncommonly mares looked so well on return home from their holiday that their owners could scarcely recognise them. Every year Carlton won new business from customers who had sent mares to top-class stallions at other establishments only to discover they had been kept in paddocks which were nothing more than worn-out dust-bowls, as a result of which they came home looking like hat-racks.

Except for visiting mares, Sam was rarely called to Carlton, for Tom was virtually his own vet. He had a peculiar gift for nursing sick animals and had his own methods of treating wounds. For example, he was a strong believer in household paraffin, provided it could run free. One horse whose flank had been ripped open was a notable case. Doctor Bill happened to be staying on holiday with Jim and said Littler would have to be sent for at once. Instead Tom threw paraffin at the wound and bound it up. It healed perfectly, whereas veterinary stitches would have been visible evermore – but of course, "It's no good pouring paraffin into a hole," as he commented to his brothers.

The only occasion when he was driven to seek a third opinion in addition to his own and Sam's was brought about by a stallion that developed a stiffness in his hindquarters which they could neither diagnose nor relieve. So W S King arrived in great ceremony from London. He was the best-known heavy-horse vet of his day and numbered among his clientele the famous geldings of the Mann, Crossman and Paulin brewery stables. He injected a new wonder-drug unknown to lesser men. His fee was £25 and Jim was appalled. Tom was reassuring. King had become aware that the Carlton intelligence network was such that, when he next needed to find the best available geldings for the brewery, the most efficient and economical way of getting exactly what he wanted was to ask the Forshaws to do so.

We have now arrived at the end of the season, which is where this review began. How had the two-year-old recruits shaped up in their initiation ceremonies? In 1933, they proved to be a mixed but generally mediocre bunch, which is why that year may be taken as an illuminating sample. King of the Realm and Silver Crown 3rd were lackadaisical failures. Judgment was reserved on Carlton Tatton Friar, but it was eventually decided not to apply for him to be licensed in 1934. That left four. Brilliantine put in three full seasons and was then sold. The Leader 2nd finished after 1938, when he was seven. In 1939, Radiation was standing at home and Grand Master 4th likewise, except for visits as substitute to the North Norfolk society for four days in June and to the Rotherham society from 18th of that month to the end of the season. Their fate in 1940, as of all stallions everywhere, was destined to depend on considerations other than their procreative powers.

14. Leaders

In a paper on breeding published in 1880 Frederic Street, co-founder with the Earl of Ellesmere of what was soon to become the Shire Horse Society, commented on the problem of finding reliable travelling grooms. "With horse-keepers at home," he wrote, "I have had little trouble. But once let such a man lead a stallion, often he becomes of little use for ordinary work. This, and the difficulty of recovering the fees, is the cause of many owners of valuable horses refusing to travel them ... I may perhaps be allowed to indulge a hope that when the education movement has had time to diffuse its influence in the formation of character among the agricultural labourers, they will see something in life nobler and higher than the indulgence of animal propensities."

His hope was fulfilled. The stallion grooms of the interwar years were vastly superior in character and habits to their predecessors half a century before. The Forshaws were especially fortunate. A few of their leaders were regular full-time men. Many of the others had been so. The remainder could be hand-picked because the prestige of the firm always ensured that there were more applications than vacancies. Even the 'own routes', on which there was no hirer to supervise them, could be confidently manned. Only in special circumstances was the groom for a Carlton horse found and supplied by a society, though this was generally the case with the Carmarthen, Caernarvon, Harlech, Vale of Clwyd, Plas Dinam, North-West Anglesey and Beaumaris people. There, an English groom would be too easily confused by names, whether of villages, farms or the multiplicity of Jones, Evans, Prices, Griffiths and Owens that owned the mares. The stallion could learn and remember a Welsh route just as easily as an English one but could scarcely be expected to read signposts or check which Mr Lewis he was obliging.

Richard normally wrote in December to men who had been booked for the following season to confirm their weekly wage, maintenance allowance, groom's personal fee payable by mare-owners and end-of-season bonus if the horse came back in good condition. Every man was expected to arrive four days before the date appointed for his stallion to leave Carlton, ostensibly to enable him to become acquainted with his charge but actually to harden him off a little. One leader, due to travel for the Wisbech Society, was overheard to say to a friend, "I'm not going a few days before – we'll be buzzing round like bees in a bloody bottle. I'll not go till the day before." He didn't, and was not offered the job the next year.

Fortunately, the season began at different times in different parts of the country. In arable districts, men liked to have their foals weaned by harvest time and so there was an early start. Cleveland Hunt was usually the first, aiming at about 22nd March, which would mean that the first few foals of the following year would be born at the end of February. The Cambridgeshire and Isle of Ely people began in the last week of that month. The Welshmen were always the latest – sometimes not until the middle of May. The main rush was in early April, and then on arrival men would have to be accommodated four to a room and two to a bed. During the four days' preparation, Richard had to discover how each groom wished to be paid – to his wife by post, in a lump sum at the end of the season, or in any other way. On independent routes, where there was no society to meet expenses, arrangements had to be made for board, lodging, shoeing and so on. In the case of a new man, it was essential that he had thoroughly grasped the contents of the Carlton rulebook and, by question and answer, that he also understood the reasons for them.

Within the confines of a single chapter, it is impossible adequately to review the Carlton stallion-leaders of the interwar period. There were too many of them. We must restrict our attention to those who were retained for many years. Of these, enough must be mentioned to be reasonably representative of all, but even enough is still too many unless we are content with the briefest of thumbnail sketches. If this treatment is sufficiently drastic, we shall then have time to dwell a little longer on just two, whose experiences will give us some guide to those of all the rest.

Pride of place must be given to Harry Whittaker, George Chapman's predecessor as foreman. During the war, while his wife had to take up work of greater national importance than making chairs, he was in the Army, but from 1919 until the next war took a horse every year – once each for the Cambridge and Isle of Ely, Crewe, Wisbech, Brigg and West Staffordshire Societies before a vacancy occurred in his own county of Lancashire, where he travelled regularly thereafter. One season, he earned £125 and was a 'made man' for months. He was a great believer in the efficacy of beer for promoting a stallion's health and vitality.

A funny-tempered man at times, he was always in a genial mood if he could collect a crowd of mill-girls to watch when a mare was served. And this could be relied upon in the Wigan area, for he and his horse over the years became an institution, the harbingers of spring. The spectators would get very excited during the preliminaries and call out such remarks as "Let's have a feel of it, groom!" And when all was over they would hang around admiringly. He was very proud of the entertainment he afforded them and on returning the horse at the end of the season would quote to his friends and former colleagues the sort of things they said, such as "If I had a horse with one like that, I would go and feel it every day". Poor Whittaker! Things did not go well with him at the last and 1939 turned out to be his final season.

Many of his innumerable small-farmer friends whose colts he broke were in the habit of exchanging sons with each other as a source of labour. But Dick Mason had never been a pawn in this game. He had come to Carlton as a boy of fourteen in 1904, on Whittaker's introduction. Three years later he travelled a stallion for the first time and did so most years thereafter as a member of the regular staff until 1914. Those early times were remembered by Jim Forshaw chiefly for a bit of bother involving him, Jimmy Ashpole and two girls up a lane. This required some sorting out, but the details have become clouded by time and are not particularly relevant. After war service, he came back, travelled for Wisbech in 1920 and then left to work for John Rimmer, a farmer and breeder of pedigreed Shires at Banks, near the estuary of the Ribble. Ten years later he moved to Cockerham and was free to resume travelling every year in the Fylde. He was an excellent leader and a good advertisement for the firm.

Five other Lancastrians deserve mention, none of them ever whole-time men. The reliable and amiable Jack Bourne, a farm worker at other times, first took a route in his home county in 1916, when he was in his early forties and new men were difficult to get. When the next war began he was still going strong and had never missed a season or proved less than wholly satisfactory. Jack Hankin, a full generation younger, started in 1930 and thereafter always had the Ormskirk district. George Proctor, who hailed from the Leyland area, had a Lancashire route in 1913 and 1914, went to war and from 1919 led 21 times for nine different Societies in eight counties – Kingston-on-Soar, Derby, Barnsley, Wisbech, Welbeck, Crewe, Brigg, Ledbury and Lichfield. This remarkable record was achieved not because he outstayed his welcome at any of them but for the opposite reason. When asked to go where he had never been before, it was to restore the Carlton reputation which had been tarnished the previous year by someone who as a result had been struck off the list by Tom; Proctor was one of the firm's trouble shooters. Jim Iles took a Lancashire route for eight interwar years, but Frank Hellen from 1916 always travelled in Yorkshire for the Selby society until 1938. The following year it decided at the last moment not to hire from Carlton, and this left him on the reserve list.

Fred Miles was thirteen when his father took him in 1907 to look at Carlton and to be examined. Tom liked his pedigree – sire, a smallholder at Branston, south of Lincoln, and good horseman; dam's sire, a farm manager at Metheringham, five miles farther south. He also liked his conformation and action – well-built if leggy (as a colt should be), and a good mover. So Fred started work, and Jimmy Ashpole told him "As long as you can get up at twenty to five, you won't want a watch here, because you'll know when to stop work. It'll be dark."

Fred worked for seven years and grew into an immensely powerful young man. Charlie Butler who first got to know him a little later said, "I don't think he knew his own strength. He could do a twelve or fourteen hour day, hard slog, and never turn a hair. Above all, he was a really fine horseman." When the war started, he went into the Army. In 1916 he was one of those released for the season, and took the redoubtable Shopnoller Drayman into Radnorshire for the Knighton and Temeside society. The next year he led the same horse for the Winslow people in Buckinghamshire. In 1918, they released him once more, and it was again Shopnoller Drayman, this time for the Kingston-on-Soar club, crisscrossing the Notts-Leicester border ('Owd Shop' wins a place of his own later in our review).

Before that season began, his eye and heart had been captivated by Mary Ann Forshaw's new paid companion, Louie Metcalf, whose father, as she used to explain, was "a farm manager against Newark". While he was away, he did a lot of writing and she did some organising. On 9th July, two days after he brought the horse back, they were married. He was not released in 1919, but was demobbed later in the year. There being no married accommodation free at Carlton, he obtained a thirty-acre small holding, Spring Farm at Sloothby, north of The Wash – in the country of old Manny Gant, who in legend was old James Forshaw's fairy godfather in the earliest days. So Tom and Jim lost a good man whom they could not have kept long on a full-time basis anyway, and their old mother lost her companion.

Fortunately, Fred's brother-in-law was available to work the holding in the season, so he travelled most years for the firm from 1920-29. He best liked his four seasons in Lancashire, for he regarded the inhabitants, as so many outside it have done, as the kindest and friendliest in England. And there, wherever he went, he found Old Forshavians. There was Will Hatherton, for example, who had been with James at Blyth – "I stayed with him one night a week on the Wigan round. Amazing old chap. Could run like a hare, even at his age." Another was Dan Norris, who kept the Eagle and Child at Billinge, and Fred stopped the weekends there. He was a man who would do anything for a laugh, and people said he was as mad as a hatter. He had not been dotty in his Carlton days, and Fred knew he was not dotty now. The newfangled charabangs would always draw up at the pub so that the passengers could have a drink with Lancashire's most eccentric landlord. Another old one was Charlie Vernon, but Fred was never keen to say much about him, except, "He was a rum lad, he was". Through his own bonhomie, Fred was perhaps the last Forshaw man ever to have a link with the old-timers of an earlier generation, where there were rummer lads than the twentieth century ever produced.

After 1929, he could no longer guarantee offering himself for three consecutive months. He just stuck to his little farm. Louie, perhaps (as she claimed) because she was the seventh child of a seventh child of a seventh child, had a remarkable gift for healing. People came to her from all over England and all quarters of the world, always of course on recommendation, because the law forbade her either to advertise her powers or charge for them. Nevertheless she probably accepted far more money than Fred ever earned.

Bill Hardy, into whose ear Jimmy Ashpole and others once peed, was another who left Carlton to be married, and he is the last we can meet who had worked there whole-time. He was a man who spoke very slowly and deliberately and moved likewise. He was once provoked into a fight with a spry little chap called Hunt, who was all round him like a bantam-cock. At last Bill happened to catch him with a heavy blow which knocked him flat. He turned to the spectators and said, "Well - I - got - that - one - home".

He obtained a job in Newark as a maltster, which fitted in well with a travelling season. From 1917 until his death in 1932 he led every year for Newark, which in his time hired some of Carlton's most famous horses. In

January 1933 its committee resolved "that the widow of the late W Hardy be given the sum of £2." This Society was founded in 1914, but long before that the Forshaws had travelled an "own-route" stallion in the district and still continued to do so in order to provide a choice – an odd arrangement which the Society surprisingly welcomed. For twenty years until 1922 this nonmembers' route was taken by Tommy Freeman, who then spent his declining days as 'boots' at the Clinton Arms where he was very popular, being particularly noted for the polite way he took people's luggage to their rooms. He was succeeded in 1928 by Cyril Wilde, a Nottingham man who worked in a hunting stables. He was sacked in March ever year and came straight to Carlton where, after the season, he was usually found something to do even in the slack time until he was wanted back by the hunt. For the final eleven years of our period his place on the route was taken by Bill Hardy's brother Tom, also a maltster. So for four years the two "lead against each other."

By the end of the war the Fieldings had ceased to play a significant part, being mostly a relic of James Forshaw's days at Blyth where their father worked for him. However, sheer force of numbers and their interest in Carlton affairs give them an historical importance, which they do not really deserve, as they were still popping up, in, or out during these two decades. The information supplied by Mr Browett, the Blyth vet, is that there were 23 of them, but Enid Oakes, who knows more about the place and its inhabitants than any others, puts the number more conservatively as "in the teens." Most lesser authorities are vague, usually just saying "Oh, the Fieldings – they was all odd-sock men," which is misleading unless we remember that Hodsock is 'against Blyth'.

They were all small, several became miners when the Harworth shaft was sunk after the war and quite a few, whether miners or not, were also stallion leaders for various owners. None of these was referred to by a Christian name, being called simply "Traveller", which is and probably was socially confusing. Only three concern us. Tommy, born in 1880, had the Retford and also the Blyth 'own routes', but in the war travelled Gainsborough and Corringham, finishing in 1920 at Blyth again, where Walter succeeded him, after having a variety of other routes previously. Charlie, the youngest, had travelled only prior to 1920, but he could have earned a place in our review of permanent staff if he had not been so erratic. He was frequently re-employed by the long-suffering Forshaws, but just as often disappeared, having found another job. He was not much good, anyway, and rarely gave his wife any housekeeping money, in return for which she rarely did any housework. Richard once visited his cottage to ascertain his future plans, if any, and Charlie wanted to show him a photograph. He had to blow a thick coating of coal dust off it – and he was the only one of the three who was not a miner.

There were four Taylor brothers. Their father Smithy Taylor used to keep a trunk under his bed and would never let his sons see inside it. When he died, the first thing they did was to go and have a look. It was full of gold sovereigns. Herbert worked in the steel works at Scunthorpe, but the other three were all employed with horses in one capacity or another. Fred could talk the hind leg off any equine. Billy had curly hair and a stutter and was also the randiest, it being commonly alleged that "every time his horse jumped, he did". It was only Jack, the youngest, who regularly led a Forshaw horse – and that was always in Cornwall. He travelled for the St Columb society in 1926 when they first hired from Carlton and did so every year thereafter. Out of season he was a colt-breaker and was also often employed by livestock auctioneers to prepare horses for sales and show them, an occupation which took him all over England.

Flannery was a peripatetic Irishman who travelled in Somerset for the Keynsham society in the Twenties, and no one seemed to know what he did or where he was at other times. If he had ever met and conversed with Fred Taylor any donkey in the vicinity would have lost both hind legs. He had a special gift for charming the ear of the society's chairman, a very important brewer who always had a rose in his buttonhole when he led the deputation to choose next year's horse. Tom and Jim used to make a fuss of this man because, although he knew little about stallions, he had the money to hire what his colleagues had selected. Coney, a Lincolnshire man who had previously travelled Cleveland, succeeded Flannery. He could have been a candidate for inclusion, with Mr Bunn the Baker and others, in the Happy Families card game for he was self-employed as a rabbit-catcher.

Harold Bagshaw of Laxton did all sorts of jobs out of the season, including harvesting and pig-killing in winter. For this he numbered the Forshaws among his customers – killing, skinning and hanging one day and returning three days later to cut up. He once went to a whist drive at Ossington, the neighbouring village, when the first three prizes were all won by Carlton bachelors and the vicar produced quite a joke about this when making the third presentation. Entering into the spirit of it all, Harold unfortunately spoiled the tone of the proceedings by calling out, "That's right, vicar. Those buggers don't come here for nothing." He travelled the local Retford district for sixteen years until 1932 when Field Marshal 6th, apparently confused about what he was trying to do, reared up and put his feet on Harold's head, which killed him. He was succeeded by Winstow from Gamston, another rabbit-catcher.

Edmund Hutchinson was a local man who had married a scrap-dealer's daughter. He was a very keen churchman and sang with great enthusiasm and a booming voice in Sutton church. He could not write or read, but this was not a handicap there because he knew the words of the hymns and canticles by heart, and most of the psalms too. It was more difficult when he took a stallion out, but Richard helped him with cards on which he had painted the names that appeared on the roadside finger-posts. By comparing the two he could find his way and soon learned it – even when based forty miles or more from home at Tilton-on-the Hill, where he was lodged by Allan Holm, one of the leading members of the Shire Horse Society and a member of its Council. Mr Holm was helpful too, and everyone liked Edmund for he was always good-natured and cheerful, though more subdued after his wife died, poor chap.

Jack Fiern, a farm worker from the Beverley area, was quiet, conscientious and capable. Throughout the Thirties he travelled his home district, as in prewar

'Field Marshal's' Route.
As near as possible).

Monday. Egmanton, Weston, Skegby, Marnham, Fledboro', Ragnall, Dunham, Darlton to High Brecks.

Tuesday. East Drayton, Stokeham, Woodbeck, Treswell, Rampton to bait, Laneham, Cottam, N. Leverton to Mr. G. Needham

Wednesday. Woodbeck, North and South Leverton, Fenton, Sturton to bait, Wheatley, Clayworth to White Hart.

Thursday. Hayton, Clarborough, Welham, Little Gringley, Grove, Headon, Upton, Askham to Mr. White, Field House, Markham Moor.

Friday. Rockley, Milton, West Markham, Tuxford, Bevercotes, West Drayton, Elkesley to Robin Hood.

Saturday. Haughton, Bothamsall, Walesby, Boughton, Laxton to Mr. P. Maddison's for week-end.

GOOD FRIESIAN BULL CALVES (from great Milking Cows) FOR SALE at Farmer's Prices.

Owners—JAS. FORSHAW & SONS, CARLTON-ON-TRENT, Newark.

Forshaws' Shire Horses
SEASON 1932.

Shire Stallion
'Field Marshal 6th'
40076.
This Horse has Government Licence for 1932.

Owners—JAS. FORSHAW & SONS,
CARLTON-ON-TRENT- Newark

TELEGRAMS :	TELEPHONE :
SUTTON-ON-TRENT.	SUTTON-ON-TRENT 3.

STATION : CARLTON-ON-TRENT.

WHARTONS, STUD PRINTERS, RETFORD.

'FIELD MARSHAL 6th,' 40076
BROWN. 6 YEARS. 17 hands 2½ ins.

Prizes—1st Reserve Champion Huntingdon County. 1st and Champion, Isle of Ely Society. 2nd Peterborough. 1929 Reserve Number S.H. Show, London. Foaled 1926.

Sire—' Field Marshal 5th,'' 35627, owned and bred by H.M. King George. Twice 1st and Champion, London and Gold Cup Winner.

  g Sire—' Champion's Clansman,' 29211, the noted Sire, also Gold Cup Winner, London and Champion.

  g g Sire—' Childwick Champion,' the famous Sire.

    Dam—80082 'Winnie' by 'Tatton Royal William,' 25690, by ' Tatton Friar,' 21953, a great Sire.

  g Dam—84781 ' Minnie ' by ' Eastern Freemason,' 20452, by ' Stonewall.'

  g g Dam—35756 ' Earith Lady ' by ' Somersham Hatherton,' 15359.

Field Marshal is a rich dark brown, standing 17½ to 17.1 high ; with feet and joints of the right kind. Knees and Hocks near the ground, clean, flat and hard, he has a great presence ; fine crest, deep shoulders made right for the collar, with a back, ribs and middle that people often talk about but seldom see ; fit to get horses for brewers, railways, corporations, contractors or agriculture ; and see his breeding :—

His Sire, ' Field Marshal,' comes from the Royal Stud at Sandringham, he having twice won Champion, London, and by ' Champion Clansman,' also Champion London, and

' Childwick,' ' Champion's ' best son. His lines are famous in the Fens—' Winnie,' by ' Tatton Royal William,' by the famous ' Tatton Friar,' and g Dam by ' Freemason,' by ' Stonewall,' a great winner in his day, so it is no lottery to breed from ' Field Marshal,' for his is the best blood going. He is the sort wanted to fill the shafts to-day, something to fill the harness and pay the rent and leave you good fillies to keep for brood mares.

Groom—H. BAGSHAW.

Terms and conditions on which Mares are accepted to this horse or substitute—
Service Fee .. £2 10 0 each Mare.
Two or more Mares .. £2 2 0 each Mare.
N.B.—Mares barren to our Horses from Season 1931, and whose 1931 Fees are paid, (if still in same owner's hands) will be charged a fee of £1 5 0 for 1932 services for such mares.
All Mares tried to be paid for.
All fees to be paid by June 24th, 1932, to Groom who will give a printed receipt.
Groom's Fee, 3 -, at time of service.
No Mare served twice within 11 days.
Groom to decide when Mares are fit for service.
NOTICE.—J.F. & Sons will not be responsible for any accident to Mares being tried or served, or from any other cause, and upon these conditions only are mares accepted to this horse ; therefore they are at their owner's risk. Should this horse become incapacitated a substitute will be provided and must be accepted.
No business on Sundays.
The Groom is not in authority to alter these terms.
To secure foals have mares cool in stable when the horse calls.

Fig. 37/38 Field Marshal 6th card for 1932, the year he accidentally killed Harold Bagshaw.

days his father had done. Another quiet Yorkshireman was Fotheringham, who travelled Wetherby all through the same decade. The only memorable thing he ever said was on the day when he first came for interview. He was a little chap, and Richard said to Tom, "I wonder if he can carry a sack of corn?" Fotheringham overheard this, and said, "I can carry two." And he could.

Tommy Franklin was a marvellous stacker. He would come back after the season and build a foursquare stack, absolutely perfect, without any markers. From 1905 and perhaps before, he had travelled for the Newport Pagnell society, but after 1920 took a number of varied routes including Stanford-in-the-Vale, Brockenhurst and Huntingdon. Another good stacker was Peacock from the Wisbech area, who led for his local society and the Huntingdon one for thirteen years. And so the list could be continued – but must not. All, in Richard's words, were "good men", including Heritage who in seven years travelled in five different parts of England.

Now to George Linney who led a horse possibly longer than anyone in history. Born on 24th May 1881, he attended the village school at Westborough, a mile or so to the east of the Great North Road between Grantham and Newark, until he was 13. His elder brother was already working for James Forshaw, but he himself found employment on a local farm at 9d a day. Here he gained some experience of handling a stallion and when almost 21 was taken on as a travelling groom by W and J Thompson of Desford, near Leicester. He was given a seven-year-old called Cotheridge Swell which they had bought from Lord Rothschild and took him to the Bridlington district. He did three more seasons for the Thompsons in various parts of the country, in the mean time marrying Annie, who had been a domestic servant for five years and a housekeeper for two. He was now self-employed, specialising in contract work as a hedger and ditcher. By this time his brother was one of the many Forshaw-trained men who had left Carlton to seek promotion elsewhere and was now with Lord Iveagh, in due course becoming his stud-groom.

In 1906, still living at Westborough, George moved into Shire House, for which he invented the name, and switched his allegiance to the Forshaws. He planned and got approval for an independent route based upon his own house, which had a stable at the side and a nice little yard for the stallion to serve any mares brought along on a Saturday afternoon or Monday morning.

He was six feet two in height and very thin, and his meticulous honesty and serious attitude to life found expression in a long and mournful face. A quiet man, he travelled his route year after year. Nothing, even the war, was allowed to interrupt the tenor of his seasons until Shopnoller Drayman created a literally hair-raising incident in 1923 (Since this reveals more of Drayman than of Linney, the story of it must come later). Undeterred, he resumed the following season, walking the same old route of about 70 miles a week from the second week of April to the first one in July. At other times of the year he harvested and hedged and ditched and was very steady about it all. Every Sunday he was a bell-ringer at All Saints.

If one year is like another, it does not matter which we choose as a sample,

Fig. 39 George Linney with Shopnoller Drayman, 'the horse that bit father', in 1923 – the only season that George was never able to complete.

as long as we avoid 1923. Perhaps 1935 is ideal because it ended in a minor and atypical, though brief, contretemps. This was the first of three seasons he led Boro' King Cole. The fee was £2-10-0, or £1-5-0 for mares that had been barren to the horse he had the year before. The season began on a Tuesday (9th April) and so that day of the week may be taken as a sample within this sample year. 'Tuesday mares' – that is, mares which were first served on a Tuesday, though perhaps on some other day of the week later – eventually numbered 21, and they belonged to 14 different people. Mrs Ablewhite's brown mare at Kilvington which had failed to conceive the previous season was miraculously 'stopped' on the very first day of operations, but her old brown one, which had a foal at foot, was served four times without any luck. The Rev George Staunton was more fortunate. His brown maiden filly conceived at the first attempt (7th May) and his barren grey mare was got in foal the third time. The horse covered the twenty-one mares 39 times altogether, on only 12 Tuesdays, none coming to him in the last week.

Taking the season as a whole, 123 mares were brought to the stallion and George therefore qualified for an extra 23 florins (totalling £2-6-0) added to his pay in addition to pocketing 123 half crowns (£15-17-6) in the way of groom's fees. The stallion's reward was a total of 229 services, averaging three a day in a slightly shortened season. These he performed with great verve and he was helped by their being spaced out fairly comfortably, since the middle of May was not quite so hectic as usual.

Like all grooms travelling independent routes, Linney was responsible for collecting the service fees. Richard had to make certain that the money handed in was correct to the last shilling. The total of cheques, cash and list of fees still owed by stubborn procrastinators had to correspond with the service book. If a man were let off a pound, he would tell the others, and so it would spread. A shortage would become normal. A pound a head this year would become two or three the next. Dishonesty would permeate all the routes and a healthy business would soon become unsound – all because of what started with a pound short. If a man was genuinely in error it was a different matter to give him something privately afterwards, but only after he had first squared things up.

This year George was £5 short. With him, that in itself was a sensation. He tried all his pockets. "I knew it was all right last night," he kept saying. "I checked it all. I had it then." Richard knew he would have done, and they both went through his pockets and then almost dismantled his clothes. A crumpled note was eventually found between a pocket and its lining. That put George straight and, since he was entitled to the £5 'present' for bringing his horse home in good shape, Richard straightened out the note and paid it back to him.

15. Customers

On the second Saturday in April at Hothersall's Horse Repository in Preston there was always a parade of those stallions which were due to travel their various routes in Lancashire. Farmers gathered in great numbers and the owners or grooms backed up their sales talk by distributing cards ad lib to potential customers – and to any of the small boys who were believed when they claimed that they wanted one "for Dad." Collecting these was an esoteric variant of the universal passion for cadging cigarette cards depicting such sporting heroes as Dixie Dean (Everton) or R E S Wyatt (Warwickshire) and W R Hammond (Glos) of England.

The Carlton four were never there. They were shown at a pub. This segregation would have been a fatal mistake for lesser-known proprietors but for the Forshaws it was good publicity. No one would make up his mind in favour of another horse until he had seen theirs – and talked to Mr Tom, Mr James or Mr Richard, two of whom were always personally in attendance.

The 1931 parade was something special. Six weeks earlier, both the London Show champions had been Lancashire-bred animals and both were the offspring of Carlton stallions. What is more, each came from a line of mares all similarly sired. The four-panelled cards handed out by Whittaker, Bourne, Iles and Hankin made much of this and the reverse side of one panel bore a special message under the heading:

LONDON SHIRE SHOW
GREAT VICTORIES FOR CARLTON HORSES AND
THEIR STOCK
BRAVO LANCASHIRE!

Lancashire is to be congratulated on producing both the Supreme Champion Stallion and the Supreme Champion Mare at the 1931 London Show. They both have generations of Carlton blood in them and their respective breeders and their fathers have always been clients of ours for sixty years. Messrs Wildman and Newhouse have a well-earned reward for their perseverance. The secret of it all is

USE FORSHAWS' HORSES
BE IN THE FRONT
DON'T GET LEFT

As usual the card was also dotted with other mottoes, such as "BRED RIGHT AND MADE RIGHT"; "WEIGHT, SIZE, SOUNDNESS AND GOOD BREEDING"; "THE SORT THAT WIN AND SELL"; and the exhortation to aim for real weight and power, "KEEP THE LURRY IN VIEW".

The other 'own routes' – principally five in Nottinghamshire, two in Yorkshire and Linney's Grantham round which crossed a boundary three times a week – were also dependably profitable. All twelve had one great advantage,

THE SHIRE STALLION
BIG GUN 41569

Will parade on Monday, 6th April, at St. Ives,
12 o'clock mid-day.   His route will be as
follows :

Subject to variation :

Monday—Abbots Ripton, the Raveleys, Upwood, Wood-
walton ; stay the night at Mr. R. J. Goodliff's
Farm, Monk's Wood.

Tuesday Alconbury Hill, Alconbury, Stukeleys, Brampton
Hut, Brampton ; stay the night at Mr. George
Lenton's Farm.

Wednesday—Buckden, Offord, Diddington, Southoe,
Little Paxton, Cross Hall, Hail Weston ; stay the
night at Mr. R. F. Aubrey's Farm.

Thursday—Eaton Ford, St. Neots, Eynesbury, Abbotsley,
Eltisley, Graveley ; stay the night at Mr. E.
Ashcroft's Farm.

Friday—Debden Farms, Lattenbury Hill, Hilton, St. Ives,
Needingworth, Bluntisham ; stay the night at
Mr. Rose's Farm.

Saturday—Colne, Somersham, Fenley, Warboys, Broughton
Abbots Ripton ; stay week-end at Mr. Favell's
Farm.

Leave each morning about 9-30

For Nominations apply to :
  CAPT. B. NEWTON, ST. IVES.
  MR. WILLIAM FAVELL, ABBOTS RIPTON.
  MR. R. F. AUBREY, HAIL WESTON.
  MR. S. V. EKINS, ST. NEOTS (Tel. St. Neots 20).
  MR. W. E. PITTUCK, 18, HIGH STREET,
    HUNTINGDON (Tel. Huntingdon 29).

HUNTS. CHAMBER OF AGRICULTURE
SHIRE HORSE SOCIETY.

Season 1936.

The Shire Stallion
BIG GUN
41569.

Hired by the above Society from :
MESSRS. FORSHAW & SONS,
·CARLTON-ON-TRENT.

On view at St. Ives Market,
MONDAY, APRIL 6th, 1936.

W. Goods & Son, Printers, Huntingdon.

Big Gun 41569.

BAY.   17.1 hands.   FOALED 1931.

Sire—" FULBECK " 39708.

g Sire—"ROYCROFT COMING KING I."

Dam—120934 "JEWEL" by "LINCOLN WHAT's
WHAT II" 25813.

g Dam—85601 "LUCY" by "PRIMLEY CHAMPION"
29735 by "TATTON DRAY KING"
23777.

A Real Stallion.

BLOOD WILL TELL.

This massive horse has great feet, flat bone
and good joints with excellent middle piece
and is of good breeding.

Rules.

1.— The Society will not in any case be responsible
for injury or accident to Mares.

2.—Any Mare tried and not ultimately served will
be charged for as if served.

3.—In the event of Big Gun being unfit for work,
a good substitute will be provided, which
must be accepted by Nominators.

4.—Nomination Tickets must be handed to the
Groom on the occasion of the first trial or
service.

Fee :
£2 15s. 0d. per Mare.
(Including Groom's Fee and Subscription to
Society).

Payable on or before June 30th, 1936, and must be
paid to the Groom or sent direct to the Secretary.

FOR ROUTE SEE OVERLEAF.

Fig. 40/41 When a horse was hired by a society, the card did not require the usual 'blurb'.
Big Gun's performance did not match his size and Tom was happy to accept an offer to buy
him after this season, his third.

in that it was Tom alone who decided what horses should take them. Only if he
chose the wrong sort of horse for a district would there be a poor return, and he
never did that.

The 'clubs' on whose behalf the majority of the stallions necessarily
travelled, were a different matter. Selection committees had to be shown

something like eight horses, because that is what they expected. They might delay a decision until they had been elsewhere. Even if they had horses from Carlton for ten years in succession, there was no guarantee that they would do so this time. It was essential to have enough stallions to show to even the last lot of visitors (for whom it might be their first visit to the stud), but to have more left than had been planned to stand at home or go out as substitutes when the season began would have been a drain on the profits earned by all the others. Even when a contract had been signed for the hire of a stallion, it was always possible that the secretary, at the end of a poor season, would be asking for a rebate to prevent its bank balance going into the red.

So far as the breed in general was concerned, these hiring societies had now become the chief instrument for improvement. The number of wealthy landlords who kept a top-class stallion for their tenants had been decimated after the war and their place had been filled by these self-help clubs.

The history of the Mobberley society in Cheshire provides a good example of this social revolution – and of the Forshaw brothers' skill in taking advantage of it. From 1880 onwards, Earl Egerton of Tatton had always made his choice stallions available in the locality at very modest fees, but after his death in 1909 the stud was dispersed. The society was at once formed to fill the gap and adopted the practice, now becoming increasingly rare, of holding a show and offering a premium to the winner, which would then be hired. In 1925, the prize was £500. Knottingley Wonder won it for the Forshaws, and Tom immediately said, "You can have him for four hundred". His brain had not softened, as people thought. He knew very well that, during that time of depression, it would be difficult to fill a hundred nominations. He was proved right. 72 mares were served at 5 guineas. His generosity had reduced a certain loss to £22 The Mobberley people thereupon abandoned the idea of fixing a premium before they knew what horse could be got for the money. Without bothering to look at the horses of any rival establishments, they sent a selection committee to Carlton and hired Lincoln What's Wanted II for the next year at 400 guineas and he rewarded their enterprise by winning the London championship six weeks prior to the start of the season. He served 97 mares at the same fee as his predecessor, and showed a profit of £59-5-0 for the members, who hired the most expensive Carlton stallion available for the next ten years after that. In this long term, the £100 had come back with interest.

Some societies were remarkably loyal to the firm, partly because of the wide choice it offered and partly because of Tom's value as an adviser before and after the season and as godfather to any horse sired by his stallions. The Horncastle society hired from Carlton every year in the two decades to 1939 and so did the Cleveland Hunt, which on eight occasions took two horses. The Selby and Newark societies missed only one year, Saffron Walden two (but twice had two horses) and Brigg three, once taking two. Among the newer converts, Scarborough and Keynsham both hired every time from 1925, St Columb from 1926, Stapleford from 1928 and, from 1929, the enormous Rydale society which had 45 Carlton stallions in those eleven years, including a record six in 1938. But nothing could be taken for granted. The Bedfordshire society, which had been a customer from time out of mind, went elsewhere in 1926 and five times in the Thirties. Huntingdon, beginning its connection in 1927, was not a customer in 1933.

In some clubs, the secretary was a farmer-member, but mostly he was the local auctioneer. The principal farmer was usually the chairman and the local bigwig president. The County Livestock Officer, always attending Annual General Meetings, was available for advice, even if he knew less about horses than some of the members. In accordance with the Ministry's model rules, there was a management committee of eleven and a four-man stallion selection subcommittee. This quartet would be given a list of studs to visit and choose the best horse available within the society's means. It was good news if Carlton was on the list, for it was celebrated for its hospitality. None other matched it. Tom and Bessie were truly shocked when one group told them in confidence of a rival stallion-owner, a very important sort of man, who had actually allowed them to await his presence in a fireless office while he devoured his lunch in the dining-room. The Forshaws' reputation was such that many selection committees were told to examine the horses before accepting refreshment. They rarely obeyed the instruction in its entirety, usually taking one or two somethings first.

The number of such groups visiting Carlton was extremely large – and not simply because there were so many stallions there. Regular customers came every year, even though they intended to have the same horse as before, and

Fig. 42 Carlton was a popular destination for charabanc outings. Mr Dowling's party, 85 in number, admire Lincoln What's Wanted II, the 1926 London champion.

Tom knew they did. Many other deputations arrived because it was *de rigueur*: a decision to hire from somewhere else, they persuaded themselves, was then better-informed. In any case it was a good day out. Bessie was philosophical about this. After all, if you keep a shop, you must let people walk about in it and enjoy themselves.

There were different types of stallions for different districts – the heaviest and hairiest for Essex, clean-legged ones for Cleveland, smaller horses for Wales, the lightest for Devon, and so on. Therefore, the day before a deputation arrived the most suitable ones were put in certain boxes. Great judgment and foresight was needed in this. For example, it was of no use to let people see a horse which would be too expensive for them. And it was necessary to keep in mind the requirements of committees yet to come. Tom could quite easily have made his own selection for all potential customers in a way that would please them and at the same time spread the resources of the stud to the firm's best advantage. The art of it was to get as close as possible to this situation even though each committee persuaded itself that it had come to its own well-reasoned and informed decision.

There were a few boxes where the floor was a couple of inches or so above the level outside. No stranger would ever notice the difference, but if a groom was instructed to put a horse in one of these, he would know immediately that the next committee would be viewing it. Similarly the yard where the stallions were shown was very slightly cambered – not sufficiently to be obvious, but spectators' feet were just a little lower than the horses' in the middle. A little bit of new gravel always enabled the groom to put the stallion's forelegs exactly where they had to be, and he had to stand him facing into the wind. Even the order in which, say, six or seven were paraded before any group was important. That naturally varied for psychological reasons. It might be a good idea, for example, to produce last of all the one which Tom really wanted a committee to choose – or perhaps last but one, with a quite unsuitable horse to follow him.

There were ways and means of emphasising a stallion's points and passing the worst off unobtrusively. If he went wide behind, he would be walked only ten yards or so away and ten yards back. Before the visitors had time really to notice anything, he would be turning. Then Tom would probably have him walked in a circle, saying "You can appreciate this one better broadside on". If he had previously instructed the groom to do something odd, to distract attention from some other defect, he would pretend the man was disobeying orders, or being incompetent, and say with a shrug "You cannot get men to do what you want nowadays".

If a stallion was a rather 'dopey' one and would look better if gingered up, he would tell the groom what to do before bringing him out for inspection. There would be a commotion, and he would say, "What the hell is going off now?" and rush in. Then the groom would bring the horse out, and Tom would be expansive about what a lively one it was, "but perfectly safe in the hands of a good man". Perhaps someone would want to have a good look at a foot, possibly to show he knew a thing or two about feet. There might be a gutta percha filling in it. Before he could see this for himself, Tom would say, "Whatever is this in here? This shouldn't be here" and scrape some of it out and quickly put the foot down. He'd make a joke of being so careless as to show a horse when there was something in its foot, and everyone would inevitably forget to have a good look after that.

A stallion having been eventually decided upon, the party would then repair to the Stud House to enjoy a lavish luncheon with plenty to wash it down. The secretary of the Barnsley society, whose area extended to the southern outskirts of Leeds, was present every year and, when eating and drinking well, always uttered sayings and saws. One of his favourites was "All the girls in 'Unslet is 'Unslet girls", by which he meant to praise the morality of their mothers. In case anyone was fatuous enough in the course of the meal to suggest a rerun of the morning's parade, "just to make certain", Tom would invariably find opportunity to express regret, in confidence, that they had infallibly chosen the best horse that he was free to offer them. This would successfully restrict his visitors to just going to his box and looking at him once more on his slightly elevated floor where in their rosy vision he looked even more impressive than before.

On one occasion, amid the banter and bonhomie that prevailed between four tipsy visitors and three teetotal Forshaws, Jim accepted a challenge to run a hundred yards against a member of a deputation. As he was sixty then, Tom was disapproving, and said afterwards, "Never do that again, James." On another visit, the Brigg people, who had come in a chauffeur-driven limousine, found it was becoming very foggy and were worried about getting back. But the secretary, an auctioneer and Methodist local preacher unaccustomed to malt liquor, would have none of that. He used his authority. "I'm the best bloody preacher on the circuit," he said, "and we won't go until I say so." This so convulsed his colleagues that they forgot the fog and stayed another merry hour.

When a society's management committee had confirmed the deputation's choice, which was inevitable because only the four had seen what was available, contracts had to be exchanged. These were based on the model form issued by the Ministry, but no two were identical since the agreed fee might be inclusive or exclusive of responsibility for paying the groom, rail expenses, veterinary attendance and medicines, shoeing, stabling and keep. Like other reputable stallion owners, the Forshaws also offered £10 or even £20 in prize money for the best colt and filly foals got by the stallion. For this purpose an autumn foal show was either organised by the society or incorporated in the local one-day agricultural event. This inevitably took place anything up to two years after the contract was signed and was not actually included in it, but the promise was honoured even if, in the intervening year, a horse had been hired from elsewhere.

Sometimes stallions were let to private individuals. The most frequent was Mr Cave, agent to the Piddington Estates in Northamptonshire, who hired a Carlton horse eleven times from 1920. When he was young and new, Richard was once in the yard there, and Cave said to him, "Hey, boy, come here". So Richard went there and was given half-a-crown, because of his good manners. T C Parke, agent to Lord Middleton at Birdsall, hired three times and Sir Herbert

Leon of Bletchley Park twice. These and others represented those landowners who still kept a stallion to benefit their tenants and the neighbourhood in general, except that on these occasions they had to hire one instead.

Reuben Covill, in the Ely district, was a stallion owner himself, but one year needed an extra horse and another time hired a substitute from Carlton part-way through the season. Eli Patchett, a Bradford wool merchant, regularly bred from his pedigree mares and usually kept a stallion, but in 1928 he had one from Carlton. Since he liked to be involved in morning activity at his stables, his shirts had detachable sleeves and Richard was much impressed by the speed with which these could be re-fixed by press studs when it was time to go to the office. Sam Jepson of Gunthwaite Hall Farm, Penistone, hired six times, it being his custom to have a stallion from somewhere or other every year to offer a little healthy rivalry to the Penistone and District society's horse.

The Martin brothers, Horace and Heber, of Littleport, near Ely, were personal friends of the Forshaws and had been the tallest men ever to enter the yard at Carlton until Heber's son began to come as well. Of the same age as Richard, he had reached a record height while at The Leys and the achievement was marked by a school half-holiday. Unlike Richard, he had been allowed to proceed to Cambridge before settling down to farming. The Martins always kept a stallion of their own at the Willow Rows on the west bank of the Great Ouse. On this deep soil their father Joseph had bred many meaty mountains of fenland flesh such as his celebrated Goliath, foaled in 1876 – son of Hercules, son of Rowell's Heart of Oak, son of Taylor's Heart of Oak, son of Glory. He had been a member of the inaugural committee of the breed society in 1878, was a steward at the first London Show in 1880, took a prominent part in the heated and often hilarious debates which eventually resulted in the English Cart Horse Society being renamed the Shire Horse Society, served on the Council for eighteen years, and died in 1913. Of his sons, Heber had by 1925 set up an all-time London record by acting as steward seventeen times. Gentlemen farmers of the finest type, they were stalwarts of the breed society.

In the Twenties and Thirties the massive Martin stallion thumped his way round the district in competition with the Cambridgeshire and Isle of Ely society's horse. However, sometimes Horace and Heber had to hire, and then they came to the Forshaws. In the 1920s there were three years when the society and the Martin stallions were both from Carlton. Other years, they might require a substitute, and he would be from Carlton also. For example, of their seven homebred mares in the 1939 stud book two were by their own horse Ouse Bridge Prince, one by Carlton Sir Edward which they had hired for sixteen days to give the Prince a rest, three by the society horse Carlton Grey Bulwark, and one by The Leader II, sent from Carlton to take over temporarily when Bulwark had trouble with an over-extended penis. In the 1939 season itself, the Martin horse became exhausted and on 15th May Carlton Trade Mark was sent in response to an SOS.

A private hirer of great note on a single occasion was G R C Foster of Anstey Hall, Trumpington. The Forshaws had gone out of their way to help him establish his stud at the end of the war, especially in supplying their own employee 'Jack' Johnson as his head man. In the seventeen years from 1920 until his death in 1936, George Foster won 101 awards at the London Show. The Anstey Hall triumphs included three successive championships (1924-1926) for Erfyl Lady Grey, the heaviest and best mare in Shire history, and three for Bower Winalot in 1932-1934. When Foster brought Jack to Carlton and hired Statfold Nulli Secundus for 1930 to fill an unexpected gap, it was pointless to practise the usual salesmanship routine, for Jack had grown up as part of it.

Henry Battye of Holmfirth, farmer, former quarry owner and diamond in the rough himself, hired a stallion every now and again. He also came to buy calves on occasion and timed these visits so that he could gather the excellent Carlton mushrooms into two huge bags he brought for the purpose. Unabashed at having failed to ask leave to do so, he would struggle to Richard's door with these bulging containers, to which he made no reference, in order to say to Ida, "Well, goodnight Mrs Forshaw, I'll be off now." The Notts fungi were for sale in the West Riding on his return home. But when he set his heart one day on five enormous mangolds, which he hoped to display at a penny a look for charity, he did ask permission, and was right to do so. After all, mangolds are viewed by the law in a very different light from mushrooms.

Of those customers who brought or sent mares to be served as outpatients, there is room here for only two. When Bar None had come to Carlton with Tom in 1887, while the rest of the stallions were still at Blyth, one of the first to patronise him was E H Nevile of Skellingthorpe. Educated at Eton and trained at Cirencester, he was a gentleman farmer in name and reality. He was then 35 and had been hunting for twenty years and breeding pedigree Shires for four. The following year he began an address to the Collingham Farmers' Club with the words, "There has come to reside in the locality a gentleman whose name for Shire horses is known not only throughout England but also throughout the great Continent of America", and then proceeded to give James a particularly gracious welcome. For over thirty years thereafter he never failed to have his mares walked to Carlton and was rewarded by a constant succession of excellent foals. Perhaps the best was a colt called Lincoln Lion (by Nailstone Coeur-de-Lion, out of a mare by Bar None) which the Forshaws bought for 600 guineas and exported to 'Boonus Airs'.

However, Edward Nevile was best known to the Carlton staff for his one monumental and long-protracted failure. In 1891, James had sold him a yearling daughter of Blyth Echo, bred in Lancashire. He called her Echo and she grew to an enormous size. Though possessing very short legs, as a proper Shire always did, she stood almost 17.3 hands – taller than nearly every stallion of the day. Yet it was not this, but her massive bulk that marked her out from any other. She produced a foal when she was four, but then put on so much flesh that, in accordance with the wise law of nature, she never had another. This was not for want of trying both by her, by the biggest and widest stallions available at Carlton and by Mr Nevile, whose obsession with achieving the impossible became so fixed that she visited Carlton two or three times a year until she was nearly twenty. All this was now past history, but the legend of her fruitless lasciviousness and her vast proportions lived on. It is a pity that Mr Nevile never had her weighed – even if only to prevent her hugeness from continuing to increase in the mind's eye after her death. One thing seems certain, though; surely, no other mare in history can have enjoyed so many half-price seasons and so many free returns. Had she remained in her native Lancashire, her encounters with the Forshaw 'own route' public stallions would have caused the local girls' eyes to pop out of their heads. Edward Nevile, incidentally, had in 1920 just retired from breeding Shires.

In the spring of 1925 Canon Francis Hanmer Webb-Peploe, Vicar of Christ Church, Cheltenham, nationally prominent as a pillar of the Evangelical party in the Church and strong opponent of anything that smacked of Romish practices, was spending a few days' holiday with his daughter Gwen, who had taken up farming. In electing to accompany her when she took her three-year-old Dogdyke Bonny to Carlton, however, he seemed to have strayed out of his proper ambience and Tom immediately ushered him into the house for afternoon tea.

Meanwhile Gwen's arrival created a sensation at the stud and the news spread rapidly among the staff. Never before had a mare been brought by a woman. She took a fancy to the exceptionally masculine Carlton Wyresdale and then amazed everyone by insisting on being present at the trial and then the mating. Not only that – she announced that she would be Chapman's assistant. It was her mare and she had every right to the privilege.

As the Canon stirred his second cup of tea, he said to Bessie, not for the first time, "Wherever is that girl? I can't think where she has got to." Even Tom was unaware that she was busy encouraging the maiden Bonny to accommodate Wyresdale's great penis.

Two years later she created a public rather than a private sensation when she exhibited Bonny's filly foal in London to win 9th prize as a yearling. No lady had ever before personally exhibited a Shire in the Agricultural Hall and there was some doubt among the stewards as to etiquette for female dress. So, to please everyone, she appeared in jodhpurs, a skirt over the top and a soft hat. She remained faithful to Wyresdale in subsequent seasons and exhibited homebred fillies, winning nine small London prizes or commendation cards until she suddenly gave up in 1933 (Her father retired in 1937, but one of his successors, the Rev David Welander, was kind enough to respond to the Forshaw biographer's enquiry by asking members of the congregation at Matins on 13th December 1970 for her current address. Alas, it was a heavenly one, but many older people told him afterwards that they remembered her well as "a rather unusual person").

There were of course many thousands of owners whom the Forshaws never met and were for them simply names and signatures in a service book. If we pick out just one of these, let us keep the Canon company by reintroducing the Rev G W Staunton of Staunton Hall, Rector of Staunton with Flawborough who, as we have observed, had Tuesday mares on Linney's route in 1935. If George Linney the bell-ringer was a kind of man now rarer than in his own day, George William Staunton was a parson of a type now extinct. He had been awarded the Distinguished Conduct Medal in 1915, but after the war began farming in Australia. However, learning that a new Rector would shortly be required, he came home. The Stauntons, as patrons of the living, liked to keep it to themselves. So he persuaded the Bishop of St Edmondsbury and Ipswich to ordain him in 1924, without a degree or any formal theological training and served his diaconate year as assistant curate of Frostenden, where one would have thought the population of 500 scarcely warranted two clergymen. Soon after being ordained priest the following year, he was duly inducted and instituted into the family parish, in the diocese of Southwell. He now had the cure of 175 souls, but within a year he became also Rector of Kilvington, where there were 42 more. One of these was Mrs Ablewhite who, like him, had Tuesday mares, and was his parishioner. He was only sixty that year and was due to remain Rector until he died at the age of ninety, leaving his flock with many curious memories, such as of the morning when he forgot it was Sunday and failed to turn up at Flawborough church. The churchwardens, searching for him, found him in a field laying drains. The diocesan authorities also had cause to remember him for his outraged and vigorous opposition to the proposal to sell the 87 acres of glebe land which he farmed in addition to his own. On reflection, it has perhaps been tactless to introduce him – for ecclesiastical reasons. He would not have had much in common with Canon Webb-Peploe.

It is impossible to ascertain how many mares were put to Carlton stallions in the twenty years 1920-1939. Of the 125 local societies in England and Wales, 71 were customers 525 times. Individuals hired 29 times. 'Own routes' were travelled 213 times. Therefore, if the standard target of a hundred mares had always been achieved, their total would have been 76,700, but to form an estimate of the true aggregate we have to subtract numbers below a hundred in disappointing seasons, add those mares above a hundred in good ones – and not least all those which were brought to the stallions standing at home. A conservative guess is that the total in those two decades was 70,000, an average of three and a half thousand mares per annum.

The Forshaws would have been shocked if anyone suggested that they were dealers but Tom was inevitably and frequently buying a selling. For example, he would purchase filly foals in the autumn. He did not want them for himself, but good ones were easy to pick up during the search for colts. There were always plenty of men who had foals but needed money. Within a month or two, it was easy to sell them. A couple of attractively-coloured ones in a paddock by the drive would soon catch someone's eye.

Many would rather rely on a Forshaw to find and buy a horse for them and pay the difference than trust their own judgment on a farm, at a foal sale, a repository auction or dealer's yard. On the other hand, there were always a few two-year-olds which were too clear of hair on their legs and no one wanted them. But the Irish did and, provided they were good horses, Tom could sell them 'by photograph' (the picture being taken by the local harness-maker – it was not a Parsons job) and ship them out in a bunch.

On one occasion he was asked to look out for a grey gelding suitable for Fremlin's brewery. A man called Grassby, near Goole, had exactly the animal. He had been offering it round for £70, but the most anyone had bid him so far was £65. Tom had a look at it and asked what he wanted:

"£70."

"Right. Send him to us."

This was so prompt that the owner wished he had said £75. Nevertheless, Tom paid on the spot, which none of the neighbours would have done. He charged Fremlin's double – and told Grassby so. He also said he would not pass him on anything extra from the profit, but if he wanted a good grey mare for breeding he could have one very reasonably. The offer was accepted, and a beautiful one arrived shortly afterwards, at a bargain price.

A big profit, however, was a rarity, and not always sought. The Forshaws had a lot of dealings with the Measures family, and might be asked to look out for, say, a three-year-old unbroken gelding which they wanted for someone. So Tom would find one and charge Measures only a couple of guineas more than he had paid for it. Even that amount of profit would be reduced by 15/- for the rail fare. The point here was that the gelding would be by one of the Carlton stallions. If a man used Forshaw stallions he could sell them the produce. And if Tom did not try to make a big profit from selling on to John or Frank Measures, he was making an ally of them.

"If anyone came into the yard at Carlton," someone once remarked, "he'd soon find he'd bought a horse from Tom, or hired one." Such a man could have no complaint, except perhaps against his own surrender to impulse-buying. The horse would be a sound one, and the right one for his needs and for the part of the country where he might use it. There were always two horseboxes waiting in the siding, and any of the Forshaws could write you out a railway ticket for the horse and yourself and save you trouble by adding the cost to the account. They would have a train stopped at the station, whence you could go wherever you liked. While you were waiting for it, it would be a surprising thing if you did not enjoy the Carlton hospitality.

Jim, and in the Thirties increasingly Richard also, spent much time lecturing throughout the country to farmers' groups on almost every topic associated with the breeding, care and management of heavy horses. They were invariably reported at enormous length in the local papers and were often given two or three columns in the national farming press under such titles as 'Mr James Forshaw Gives Away his Secrets', 'The Future of the Shire: Mr Jas Forshaw's Confidence', 'Mr Richard Forshaw addresses Hunts Chamber of Agriculture', 'Mr J Forshaw discusses Shire Blood Lines', 'Mr R Forshaw on Unsound Horses'. When Jim was speaking as President of the National Horse Association, the headline was usually something like 'Mr James Forshaw on British Horses'.

Fig. 43 This drawing bore the caption "Mr Punch believes the Shire horse should be judged on its curves rather than its points". He proved his own point by making the whole picture with the aid of compasses.

The lectures were never delivered in over-technical language. For example, "From the front if you cannot see your horse's hind legs, that is what we call good enough. From the back, if you cannot see his front ones, he will do." On the subject of blood lines (studiously avoided in this book) they were usually equally down to earth. A stallion which did not always breed true but threw back to a remote ancestor of a wrong type must be got rid of. Too often, Richard said, they were sold off cheap and impressed people by having a long pedigree. "A stallion does not serve mares with his pedigree. If his fee seems cheap, be wary. For the man who uses him, a cheap stallion is an expensive mistake." Talking to the Longridge Agricultural Discussion Society, Jim said, "I know a farmer who had one of the biggest and best collections of mares spoiled, and it has taken him thirty years to eliminate the ill-effects of that one sire." Both father and son kept their lectures short and were prepared to answer questions 'about what you really want to know', until the chairman had to stop them. All this was of course excellent publicity for the firm, but they both regarded it as a genuine educational exercise.

It was not only the press which quoted the Forshaws as oracles. One would not have to travel far anywhere in England to meet someone who in conversation would boast of the time he met Mr Forshaw, by whom he usually meant Tom or, if he was an oldish man, James. Just as people today who have been fortunate enough to be presented to the Queen, a pop star, a television personality or even a leading politician always insist on recounting exactly what the celebrity said, however trivial, so they would quote Mr Forshaw. It has no doubt been ever thus. Someone must have been impressed when Mr Gladstone said to him, "I never eat nuts". If not, how would we know now that he ever said it? Old Mrs Brammer liked to tell people "My grandfather was John Ward of Sudbrook, and he got to know Mr Forshaw in this way. He was taking a load of corn to Newark and had a good cart mare. Mr Forshaw came up and said, 'That's a very fine mare you have there.'" What is significant about this is that she was talking about *old* Mr Forshaw and was quoting what he said to grandfather when Gladstone was Prime Minister. And here it is repeated once more, this time in print. "That's a very fine mare you have there" is surely just as profound and memorable a remark as "I never eat nuts".

16. Stallions

To follow the example of Mr Agriculture on his visit to James in 1887 and recite the merits of the Forshaw stallions of 1920 to 1939 would be not only impossible on account of their numbers, but tedious in the extreme. In selecting only a few, as in the case of the employees and customers, of those which left a vivid memory behind them, the aim must be to illuminate rather than glorify the Carlton enterprise.

Strictly speaking, England's Crown does not qualify in respect of date, but he claims attention before it is too late. He had been discovered in 1913 when three years old, still in the hands of his breeder and not yet even registered in the stud book. He was sent to the Fylde in 1914 and then to Doncaster, Spalding and Towcester, each time with a different groom. His enthusiastic contribution to the war effort became legendary. Sadly, no record survives of the number of mares he covered until 1918, when he was taken by L/Cpl H Wells, released from military duties for the purpose, to the Stamford district. That year he dealt with 181. How many of these came back to him a second or third time is unknown, but it may be suspected that it was only a small proportion. He was 'smittle', not just virile. Harry Wells, who had led for Carlton every year from at least 1907 until he joined up, was not released in 1919, when a man called North took him back to Stamford and somehow spoiled him, perhaps by letting him do too much. Whatever the truth of it, that was the last season for England's Crown – and it was North's only season (Harry, incidentally, took a smallholding at Sutton-on-Trent on demobilisation and only once after that, in 1923, was free to travel again. A pity. "He was a good man," Jim told young Richard, using a regular Forshaw cliché).

Tandridge Coming King, bred in the unlikely county of Surrey in the same year as England's Crown, had arrived two years before him as a yearling in 1911. Fred Miles never forgot him. "When I saw him coming in, and he had all that hair and that massive great wide behind, I said 'This one will soon make rubbish.' But I were wrong." The massive behind was an asset in his procreative efforts over eleven seasons, 1913-1924, and he earned so much money that when Jim built a house for the children's governess he called it Tandridge.

For sheer earning-power, it would be pleasing to consider Burgeon, who arrived at Carlton when five and was virtually hyperactive until, at the age of 19, someone came with cash in hand to offer him a programme much more appropriate to a very elderly horse. That was in 1911, and the date-qualification must not be ignored again. Tom, always laconic, remarked, "There is always a call for a sound horse, whatever his age".

Only especially valuable Carlton horses were insured, and those only when young, because the premium was so high. Third party cover was of course essential, but claims were remarkably rare. One stallion whose identity, though suspected, cannot now be proved was proceeding sedately along the road when he suddenly swung round, lifted a little man from his pony and dumped him on the ground with a thud. No harm was done and he was only joking.

Shopnoller Drayman, who came from Somerset at the age of two in 1913, was not a joker. He was never shown in London because he stood exactly 16.2 hands – half an inch too tall for the short-legged class, but too short to do well against bigger horses. Perhaps, in the interest of safety, this was fortunate. It is not now clear who took him to Wigan in 1914, but next year he went to the Horncastle society with a new man called Swiffen, who never led for Carlton again. Whether he took fright or joined the forces or died, or all three, is now unknown.

In 1916-1918 Fred Miles was released from military duties, as we have seen, to lead him for three different societies. "Owd Shop," he said sixty years later in the tranquillity of old age "was the best horse that ever lived. His legs was as good at the end of his days as any three-year-old. And it didn't matter how many mares were waiting for him, he'd serve them all and stop the lot. He needed mastering, though. When he got angry, he'd walk on his hind legs. And while he was doing it, he'd make a tremendous noise. Like a lion roaring. His hair was as glossy as could be. I just loved him."

"He was wicked. With a wicked horse, some folk would just shut the door on him, and be glad to. But what was the good of that? That'd leave him the master. You'd have to go in to him and let him know, as quiet as you could, that you was the master. With entires, there's only one master – you or him. With a

Fig. 44 Shopnoller Drayman again, this time with his friend Fred Miles

wild one, and an evil one, a killer perhaps, you'd have to do whatever was needed. But you could still be kind to him. You had to be, if you wanted to be his friend. And you had to be quiet. Once something frightened him and he jumped over some rails as spry as a kitten. But he wouldn't jump back, so I had to lead him round and back to where we'd come from. Then he did it again. So I took me weskit off and put it on his head backwards, with his ears sticking through the armholes. That made a good blindfold, and he was all right the third time."

Shop was hired a second time by the Kingston-on-Soar people in 1919, when Fred was not released by the Army. So George Proctor, who had been demobbed, took him over, and again in 1920. Then followed a season with Tommy Freeman, the regular Newark man, before Fred renewed the partnership on the Wigan circuit in 1922. When daily exercise recommenced that autumn, Richard's mother happened to see her son leading him up the lane and prayed for his safe return. After all, he was only just approaching his eighteenth birthday and Repton had not prepared him for this sort of experience. She had heard Tom Forshaw say that it was essential to look the horse in the eye and keep staring at him. Could the boy stare hard enough?

In 1923 Shop was allotted to George Linney. One day at the Peacock, Redmile, which was then a farm, he was in a box and George went in to get him out. Shop grabbed him by the hair and he escaped only by leaving it in the horse's mouth. It was lucky that his charge was still tied up. J Mabbutt, a farmer and good horseman, and Bill Todd, carrier and another good horseman, were there and so were a lot of boys sitting on a fence, watching. George was taken to hospital to be patched up as well as possible, but though his scalp healed he never grew hair on the top of his head again. Of all the many stallions that George ever travelled, Shop was thereafter known in his family as 'The Horse That Bit Father.'

Late that night, Tom's youngest daughter Mabel was woken up by gravel being thrown at the bedroom window. She opened it and looked out. It was one of the men shouting, "George Linney's been scalped."

The following evening, Fred Miles, travelling Royal Oak on the Wigan route, received a telegram "SEND HORSE HOME STOP AWAIT REPLACEMENT TOMORROW MORNING." When the train arrived, it was Shop! "There now," said Fred to the railwayman, "that's just what I wanted. It's my old friend they've sent me." Fred led him for the Welbeck Tenants' Society in 1924 and on the Retford route the next year. But this had to be the end. He was despatched in full state as if going to the London Show which he had never visited, on his last short journey. A year or two later, Tom Forshaw said, "Look, Fred, I have a photo here of you and your old friend, and I want you to have it." Many years afterward, Fred gave Richard a present. It was one of Shop's shoes, and Richard had it made into a useful boot-scraper.

Rickford Coming King, three years older than Shop, was also Somerset-born and the two, though unrelated, had one thing in common: their fathers belonged to the same man. Rickford Coming King was bred by Lord Winter-

Fig. 45 Like Owd Shop, Rickford Coming King was Somerset-born. A modern painting by R F Wyatt from a Parsons' photograph.

stoke, the Bristol tobacco baron (actually, of course, by George Edwards, his head man) but eight weeks before he was foaled, his sire Ravenspur, purchased the previous year by Lord Winterstoke from the King, suddenly died. King Cole VII was bought from Lord Rothschild to replace him and, used by Tom Dibble of Shopnoller, became the sire of Shop.

In 1910, Rickford Coming King won first prize among 107 two-year-olds at London. Eleven months later his owner and breeder, one of Bristol's most revered and munificent benefactors, died. Robert Heath bought the colt for 1175 guineas and took him to Staffordshire, where he spent five prolific and riotous years, concentrating in his spare time on trying to fulfil an ambition to slay Mr Heath's younger son Freddy. As Freddy rarely spoke to cart horses and spent most of his time playing bridge, he was still alive when the Forshaws took a weight off the father's mind by buying the horse in the fall of 1915 for much less than he had paid for it.

The following February, at the age of eight, he was taken to London, where he stood top of the big stallions class. He was hired by the Cambridge and Isle of Ely society, his groom being a new man called S Dockray whom Carlton never heard of again, which may or may not be significant. The next year he was beaten into second place in the class but was nevertheless chosen as reserve to his conqueror for the supreme championship, and was then let to the Bedfordshire society, where he was led by William ('Jack') Johnson. In 1918 he would have been eligible for the old stallions class, being now ten. However, in the restricted show at Newmarket, this class had to be cancelled. This did not matter because he became supreme champion anyway. Jack took him back to Bedford and in 1919 to the East Hertfordshire society. In 1920 no Forshaw horses could be shown because Jim was a judge, but the Carmarthen society had booked him and, as was usual in Wales, supplied their own groom, who probably did not know what he was in for. He was not exhibited the following year, when he went into the Fylde. Jack had now left to become head man for Foster, and so he was led by Richard Johnston of Balderstone, whom he savaged so badly that the poor fellow died in hospital.

The 1922 Show was a notable one for the old war horse. He was reserve for the championship, a dizzy height never scaled before or since by any stallion as old as 14. Furthermore, one of his own sons, Chatley Coming King (also Somerset-bred) stood second to him in the old stallions class. This son had been conceived – in a mare that herself had been born at Rickford – when he himself was only two. Among humans, it may be uncommon for father and son both to be drawing the old age pension, but if both were to be acclaimed in the same year as the fittest and most handsome men over 65, it would be unique – as this remarkable occasion certainly was.

Perhaps the most surprising aspect of it all was that Chatley was such a good specimen. Rickford Coming King's inability to father sons anywhere near as good as himself was now notorious. This is not to say that he did not have hundreds of them, and hundreds of daughters, for he remained even in ripe old age extremely fertile. His erratic performance can be perhaps put down to shortage of pedigree. His grandmothers had miserably plebeian ancestries where, no doubt, there lurked below-stairs genes which, transmitted to and through him, resulted in unpredictable offspring.

In the season following this 1922 Show, young Charlie Butler was paid the compliment of being told to take him on a return trip to the Fylde. This was an experience he never forgot. "He had a constitution as hard as anything could be and was a wicked old bastard. He stood just about 18 hands – short legs, perfect, deep through the shoulders, a big solid block, built like a rock. He was the finest specimen of a Shire I ever saw. The devil in him – that made him really something."

In 1923 he was the oldest horse in the Agricultural Hall and the oldest ever to win a first prize there. He now went on a special mission. The death of the 9th Lord Middleton, an indefatigable apostle of Shiredom, had left Tom Parke, the estate manager at Birdsall, in a quandary. A new stallion was needed for the use of the tenants, and they were always offered the best available, but until matters were settled for his late employer's brother to take over, he did not want to buy. So he hired Rickford Coming King and supplied his own man as groom. Within a few weeks this poor fellow had one of his fingers bitten off and others mangled. Charlie was sent up and Mr Parke met him at the station. He said, "You just give the word, and I'll have the bugger shot. He's dangerous." For sixty hours, no one had dared go into him and he was now so desperate that he was turning frantically in circles. The blue-brick floor of his box was shining like glass. Charlie got a little water in a bucket and a little feed, and went in. Within a few days, the horse had recovered from his solitary confinement and was able to resume his work. The local leader had three weeks off, but "he had some pluck, because he came and took him over again. He said to me, 'It was my own fault, I got a bit careless.'"

The horse came home on 25th July, but his temper had now at last completely worn out. Tom just touched him with a whip. The reaction was frightening. Richard never forgot it (After all, it was his first year after leaving school). "He went back on his hunkers and laid his ears flat on his head." He was put in his box with a head collar on, and shot. Twenty years later, Tom said, "He was a show horse, if ever there was one. Paradoxical as it may sound, he was high and low, and long and short." Jim used to say he had "every link of equal strength". And Richard, fifty years on, still remembered him as "the most perfect horse I ever saw".

With the demise of Rickford Coming King, it is perhaps appropriate to record that, although the Forshaws had not competed in the "10-year-old and upward" class until 1902, the eighteenth year it was staged, they had now won ten first prizes, three seconds and two fifth prizes in a possible eighteen years (The class was omitted in the Newmarket years and Tom and Jim were judging on two occasions). This record should have been sufficient to silence anyone who suggested that Carlton stallions were overworked. London prizes were won only by those which were fresh and sprightly. What is more, three times the supreme champion of the Show had been a Forshaw stallion aged ten or over, a feat never accomplished even once by anyone else until J G Runciman, the Cambridge vet, at the very last in 1939 managed it with the ten-year-old Bower Winalot, which in its younger days when shown by the ex-Forshaw man 'Jack' Johnson had been three times champion for G R C Foster.

Generosity, bred in Montgomeryshire, was sold for £58 as a yearling in 1916 and resold the following year for £700. He then fell ill. On his recovery, Tom paid 1500 guineas for him and sent him to Lancashire with Jimmy Ashpole in 1918. The following February, he became supreme champion at the breed show in succession to Rickford Coming King. Bill Hardy then took him to Newark, where he failed to stop any of his mares and had to be substituted. It was then learned that he had left hardly any foals in Lancashire. The puzzling thing about him was that, sometimes after he had served a mare, which he always did with verve, he would immediately attack the groom. So he had to have two men, one on each side, to pull him away from whichever he had turned upon. At other times, he was perfectly well behaved. External examination revealed nothing apparently wrong with his penis and he produced semen, but the spermatozoa were all dead or deformed. The reason for the infertility was never diagnosed. Tom suspected his early illness had been some form of equine mumps, but veterinary science was not then sufficiently advanced to determine the matter. Like Rickford Coming King, he was shot and buried at home instead of joining the hanging day train.

The grey March King (1916-1923) had the distinction of being hired for a record £2,000, as we have noticed. A gentlemanly horse, he was also very popular with the mill girls when taken to Lancashire by Harry Whittaker. He was a very smittle one, too, but his importance in history is due to his extraordinary prepotency in transmitting greyness to his many stallion sons, most of which also had that power. Among pedigreed Shire foals born in 1920, 2.4% of the colts and 3.2% of the fillies were grey. By 1939, the percentages were 22.7 and 11.7. This was March King's doing.

If unbroken success, the bluest of blood and immaculate behaviour become boring, then only the essential facts must be given about Lincoln What's Wanted II (1917-1931). They are two. In 1926, he became the ninth Forshaw horse to be chosen London champion – easily a record. Twenty-seven of his sons carried on his good work of attempting to turn the whole Shire breed into male-line descendants of the famous late 19th century Harold – in the same way as the March King tribe (also of the Harold line) was trying to make it all grey.

Bradgate Premier was already six when purchased from his fourth owner at the auction following the 1929 London Show. Tom wired home to expect the arrival of the extra horse and added "MUST GO IN FYLDE". This confused the telegraph operator who in turn puzzled Curtis with "MUST GO IN FIELD". Premier had previously won minor London prizes a few times but after joining Carlton came within an ace, or a two, of being champion on four occasions. However, his claim for inclusion here is his long service, (he was still hard at work in 1939) and smittle buoyancy. To take as an example one day in May 1933, a mare belonging to Everitt Brown, secretary of the Newark society, was the twelfth he had served since breakfast. Another was expecting him next door, and he owner had been watching. When Jimmy Ashpole brought him straight away, he was furious.

"I just saw him on Brown's mare only ten minutes ago. It'll be no good unless you wait. It's a disgrace. I'll get Brown to report you to Mr Forshaw."

Jim stood his ground. "I'm not going to hang around to please you. It's late. You can bring her round in the morning if you like, before I leave. But if he takes her now and she doesn't hold, there'll be no fee." The man accepted the challenge – and in due time had to pay up.

Coleshill Inventor (1924-1926), a potential killer, was castrated before seeing a mare, but was kept on as a work horse since even after his operation he was too dangerous to sell. Chatsworth Prelate (1925-1930), bred by Mr Bullock of Great Sheepy, came into the Duke of Devonshire's possession as a yearling but was hastily sold to Carlton the next year. Joe Gaskin led him for the Cambridge and Isle of Ely society in 1928 and 1929, but he so terrified the Fareham and Hampshire members the next year that, when Joe bought him home, he was shot. Royal Warrant arrived as a foal in 1928, revealed himself as a 'nabber' the next year and at two became savage and was castrated. He was beautiful. John Measures of Dunsby bought him and renamed him Pendley Warrant – now that he was a gelding, he could be called anything anyone liked. Measures sold him to Charles Franklin, the Bedford coal merchant. In 1936, with a notice on his box "DANGEROUS – KEEP AWAY", he became

Fig. 46 The slope and The Dean's short legs make Arthur Mumford look taller than he would seem in the picture of Hawton Blend (Chapter 12, fig. 33).

champion gelding at London. This ambition achieved, Franklin was glad to pass him on to the London haulage contractor Percy Surridge, for whom he was champion gelding the next year. He brought fame to these last two owners but, if he had been given work to do on the streets, he would surely have bitten someone's arm off.

The Dean, son of Lincoln What's Wanted II, not an ecclesiastical horse, was bred in 1928 by Stanley Dean. He put in three seasons for each of three societies (the Cleveland Hunt, St Columb and Wem) in the years 1931-1939. An almost perfect specimen of a Shire, he won the London short-legs class at four consecutive shows from 1934 and might have done so in 1938 if Tom had not been judging. From 1882, when it started, to 1939 this class was held at 55 shows. Omitting the six when a member of the family was judging, Forshaw horses won first prize 29 times in a possible 49.

King George V was the breeder in 1932 of Appleton Binder and won 2nd, 5th and 6th prizes with him at London. On 11th December 1935 A C Beck, the Sandringham agent, wrote to Tom Forshaw requesting him to exhibit the horse on behalf of His Majesty at the next Show. None of the Forshaws could think why the King's illness should make this necessary. After all, though His Majesty personally drew up the breeding programme for his beloved Shires and never missed a London Show if he could help it, he was not accustomed to bring them into the ring. A family council decided that, if Richard showed the horse, it would invite comment. Tom Curtis would not be recognised as a Carlton man and was therefore told that the honour would be his. He had long dreamed of exhibiting a stallion at London and had never had the opportunity. Now this! The King's horse! Appleton Binder was immediately sent over from Sandringham to be prepared.

On 20th January the King died. Binder and the other Sandringham Shires now belonged to his eldest son. Curtis obtained 4th place for the royal horse and this was the only occasion that Edward VIII was ever listed as 'exhibitor' of a Shire. Shortly afterwards he disposed of the entire stud and also of the other species of pedigree livestock at Sandringham. This was an act which, as the Times was to recall many years later, "caused circles enjoying much influence to fear for the soundness of the King's judgment in matters of moment". With the death of George V a glory had departed from the Shire Horse world. For fifty-five years the breed Society had had no more enthusiastic and practical supporters than its first two Royal patrons. Between them they had bred a champion mare and a double champion mare and had bred *and* exhibited a double champion stallion.

In the June of 1939 J Peacock, travelling as usual for Wisbech, spotted a promising grey colt foal left by his horse of the year before, a great-grandson of March King. On his return he recommended the little creature to Richard. But by the time Tom went to have a look at him there was a war on.

17. End of the Road

Six weeks after the war began, the Ministry suspended grants to the local societies. Horses on farms would need assistance to deal with the ploughing programme, but this would come in the form of Government-procured tractors, mostly from America. The Army would not want horses this time. Next, rations were refused to stallions, although allowed for working horses.

One train from the Carlton siding carried away twenty-three horses for slaughter. Eight would have departed on hanging day in any case, but the other fifteen had been on duty earlier in the year at fees amounting to about £4,800. They fetched £3 a head, because horse flesh could not be used for human consumption. Not long afterwards, this became permissible and they would have been worth about £120 each.

The majority of hiring clubs and farmers had not shared the Ministry's view that a case could not be made for the continuation of breeding. They still wanted the stallions. Six recruits enabled licences to be taken out for 63 Carlton horses in 1940 and 36 were either let or travelled the freelance rounds. Richard had many problems in organising their transport and discovering ways and means to feed them. Jim Ashpole had left to work for Parry's pump works, but was given three months off to lead Lymm Ironclad for Newark.

On 10th May, as German forces were invading Belgium and the Netherlands, Saxby Commander was sent to the Cleveland Hunt because Enderby Radiation's penis had received a crippling kick. Paul Reynaud, the French Prime Minister, telephoned Mr Churchill on the 15th and said, "We are beaten." The same day, Lincoln Grey Lad replaced Bowden Lincoln on the Newark 'own route'. Coleshill Field Marshal, with Hankin in the Wigan district, overstretched himself and was relieved by the former Sandringham stallion Appleton Binder, who made the journey on 4th June, just as the evacuation of 338,226 troops was completed from Dunkirk.

In September a stick of bombs was dropped just beyond the bridge over the main railway line near Richard's house at Sutton. He and Ida slept downstairs thereafter and William the baby was put into a specially strengthened cupboard under the stairs at night. The Selby society, regular hirers from 1920, folded up.

Forty-six Carlton stallions were licensed in 1941 and forty in 1942, when the Government announced it would play a new tune. Grants were to be reinstated. Licences had been issued to 1,200 heavy stallions in England and Wales and these also qualified for rations, even extra ones during the covering season. One coupon would buy a hundredweight of bran and was valid anywhere. This was awkward, as it had to last two weeks. A horse would, therefore, set off on a Monday with half a hundredweight on its back and his groom had to hope he would find the other half still inviolate when he returned to base on the Saturday.

Richard and his family had moved to Tandridge, the house built in 1914 for the Misses Wigfull. May had been his sisters' governess, Jessica taught at a boarding school and Florence was married to the local grocer, Mr Woolfit. Daisy Gaskin was now Ida's daily help. Her husband Joe was leading Carlton Benefactor for the Saxilby Society – two great heavyweights thumping their weekly way round the countryside west and north of Lincoln. At Hillside, Jim, a widower for seventeen years, still had the stout Lily Bell as housekeeper. She was to prove as jolly with Richard and Ida's boys as she had been with the girls of the previous generation – provided that they conformed to her standards of child behaviour.

Jack, the youngest of the Taylor brothers, who had travelled a Forshaw stallion for the St Columb Society every year from 1926, surprised Richard at the end of this season by suddenly saying, as they were coming out of a field together, "I'm not going there again." At first he would not say why, but eventually admitted that there was a man who promised to shoot him if he ever set foot in Cornwall again. "And he means it."

"Whatever have you done?" asked Richard.

"Well I've got a woman in the family way, sir. His wife."

He had lodged once a week with a farmer's son. This son went to milk in the mornings at five o'clock and Jack would obligingly take the young wife a nice cup of tea, and then get into bed before feeding his horse.

Joe Gaskin therefore took over at St Columb in 1943. George Linney's route was abandoned and he led for Joseph Owen and Sons of Horbling, near Sleaford for a couple of years before calling it a day. He had handled stallions for just about fifty years and travelled for 43. In due course he completed his half-century as a bell-ringer, celebrated his golden wedding and died as a widower when he was 87.

In 1943, 40 stallions were licensed, and 29 were on the road. The following year the numbers were 37 and 25 respectively. Local societies were either closing down or suspending operations in the hope that things would revert to normal when the war ended. At the stud itself, George Chapman, in failing health, had gone with Elizabeth to join their son Alec at Fremlin's brewery, where he could do light duties. Tom Curtis was now foreman. Fred Wilson retired and developed the odd habit, when he went down to the village, of locking his wife in the house. It may have been from her that he got the idea, for she had always bolted doors against her bachelor lodgers to prevent their going into rooms where she did not want them. He was succeeded by a part-time man.

The Shire Horse Society which in 1941 had had to evacuate its stately home at 12 Hanover Square, where nearly all records of its sixty years' work had been reduced to pulp under four feet of water in the cellars as the result of a bomb, was now languishing in miserable suburban accommodation. However, in expectation that the war might soon be over, it planned to hold its first Show since 1939 – not in London because the Post Office had taken over the Royal Agricultural Hall, but in the Derby cattle market. It was held on Thursday, 8th March 1945 and was restricted to just three classes for stallions, for it was on

Fig. 47 Born before the second war and champion after it, Grey Spark is here at home. Photograph by G S McCann of Uttoxeter. Parsons would have wanted to paint Richard out of it.

these that the future of breeding would depend, if there was to be a future. The lovely colt foal, recommended by Peacock on returning from his Wisbech round in 1939, was now six. Richard exhibited him and, beating the other 103 present, he won the championship.

In 1946, 23 licences were taken out. Saffron Walden somehow managed to find 106 mares for Tom Curtis with Carlton Grey King, which became the last stallion in Shire horse history to achieve the century, though Grey Spark had a near-miss with 96 produced by the Pentrich and Shottle people in Derbyshire. Six other societies hired, including Keynsham, from where Flannery walked and talked his way round north Somerset as usual. One horse was hired by a private individual. The five remaining 'own routes' produced a total of 288 mares. The last two Forshaw stallions to travel in Lancashire – in this 132nd year from 1815 – were led by Jack Hankin and old Dick Mason, now 65 and walking with a stick. Dick had not lost his salesmanship skills and persuaded the genial Bernard Prescott, fourth in line from Thomas Forshaw at Dutch Barn Farm, to have his two old mares served. Though he had always used Forshaw horses in the past, Bernard had not bred from them since the beginning of the war. Dick had a young man with him to hold the horse while he merely supervised its penis. They went through this performance at intervals until the season was over, but the mares seemed to have lost the knack of conceiving. Bernard has said that he was not upset by the failure because he had only agreed to the old chap's proposal out of sympathy, which was typical of him.

Tom was now 81 and Jim nearly 73. They decided to retire. Richard made up his mind that the stud should close. This could not be done overnight. He was already committed to five societies for the following year. 1947 therefore began with eleven stallions on the books, but only the five were travelled. British Ambassador covered 86 mares at Saffron Walden, for whom Tom Curtis had now done his 28th and last season – with 21 different horses. The other four horses had an average of exactly 48 each. Aldwell Royal Conqueror, with old Cuzzy Wood, had been hired by the Holderness society. Pentrich and Shottle had Crossfields Ambassador and a man called Myers led him. Ben Midgley, who sometimes had appeared at Carlton out of season delivering hay, did his twentieth successive year for Stapleford, on this last occasion with Carlton O K. Joe Gaskin took his vast bulk and Lymm Wild Wave round the Doncaster area for the Thorne society. Then he retired, though Daisy continued as Ida Forshaw's 'daily'. While he was away, the first of Bill Forshaw's milk teeth had become loose and she said, "Come over here in the light. I only want to look at it." A sudden jerk removed not only the tooth but also, temporarily, the little boy's trust in women. Some people, like Daisy, are remembered rather for trivial incidents than for any major contribution they may have made to history.

Arthur Mumford got a job elsewhere but later retired to his Sutton home where in his old age Ida Forshaw was to take him meals on wheels. Alf, the youngest of the Ashpoles, went to work for a breeder of Percherons before taking a pub in the west country, where he was his own best customer.

Of the long-serving leaders, nearly all Richard's 'good men' had to be dropped one by one, or had dropped out themselves. Altogether, the number of Carlton travelling men – between 1920 and 1947 only, and omitting those provided by such societies as supplied their own grooms – was 161.

Grey Spark was sold during this last season and, watching him depart, Tom wept. No one had ever before seen him display emotion. This left ten stallions which, unlike the green bottles, all fell at once. With the remaining stallion harness and all other dead stock and all the Friesian cattle, they were sold by auction on 9th September, the day when Richard and Ida celebrated their tenth wedding anniversary. Coleshill Carlton had already been booked by the Stapleford society for 1948 at £275 and so Richard posted off the contract to the purchaser, Richard Sutton of Longton – only eight miles from the market place at Chorley.

Old James, who in 1888 had forecast that "one day they will not want horses" had been proved right, but his planning of the stud buildings so that they could be converted into a factory, with rail access to the very door, was unnecessary. A family limited company was formed and Richard established a new herd of cattle, fully attested, and started up afresh, with Tom Curtis as his head man. On the wall facing the railway line, the words "SHIRE HORSES" were left to continue fading away, and beside them in fresh black paint appeared "BRITISH FRIESIANS".

On 30th August 1948, Tom lost his wife Bessie in her 84th year. Bill, the doctor, who had been honorary medical officer at the London Show for many years, died in 1950. Jim, who had played tennis until he was seventy and had a saying "It's no good getting old unless you get tricky" had devoted much time and energy to affairs which have not concerned us here such as the council and committees of the Shire and Royal Agricultural Societies and as a leading judge of Friesian cattle. Surviving a stroke by nearly a year, he died in a Nottingham nursing home on 12th June 1952, at the age of 78.

In his 'eighties, Tom's declared recipe for a long life was to "say your prayers and keep your bowels open". He had his three daughters, all now married, but, bereft of his son so many years ago, regarded Richard's three as vicarious grandsons. The eldest, Bill, has written that "on a Saturday, he would practise the next morning's hymns and for years he would watch the local cricket team, and the bowlers especially would receive slightly paternalistic advice which they accepted with deference. When he became too slow on his feet to cross the A1 with safety, a hole was cut in the cricket field hedge to enable him to see the game from the dining room of his house. He was active enough to play croquet in the garden until his 89th birthday. I would play with him every Sunday afternoon in the summer. Then, after a boiled egg and buttered toast tea, we would play rummy all evening."

He duly attended the Shire Horse Show in appalling weather on the racecourse at Derby in March 1955 to maintain his record of never having missed one since the very first in 1880, when he was fourteen. There were only 34 stallions and 33 mares on view, numbers being made up by 22 geldings and three classes for horses "of Shire type yoked to a vehicle". He noted with approval that Charlie Butler won all these for Young's Brewery. On 28th September, after celebrating his 90th birthday, he was appointed referee at the National Pedigree Shire Foal Stakes, also at Derby. The judges could not agree about the top two among the twenty-seven filly foals and he was called in. Walking-stick in his right hand, upright as ever, he emerged from the ringside to loud and prolonged applause. He died on Christmas Day and they buried him at Carlton near the church where he had sung in the choir for sixty years.

Since his death coincided with the demise of the horse age, the Forshaw contribution to the vast improvement of the Shire horse as a durable and efficient source of tractive power has been quickly forgotten, especially as the points to be observed in breeding animals for pulling heavy loads no longer now apply. Of the local societies operating in 1939, five miraculously survive. The secretary of one, in response to an enquiry about the preservation of its minute books, wrote that they had all been lost or destroyed, but added the information that "before the war I understand we hired stallions from people called Foreshoe". Sic transit gloria mundi. It was as if a cricketer were to speak of a famous old-timer named W G Grease or a portrait painter to admit that he had heard of Remnant – or, for that matter, a stockbreeder to imagine that Bakewell was a tart.

As for a man's personal qualities, the most accurate judges are usually his employees. Fred Miles and Charlie Butler were first-class horsemen, candid to the point of bluntness and highly articulate. Sitting at home in retirement, Miles said, "I'll tell you what sort of man Mr Tom was. He was like his mother, one

Fig. 48 Windsor, 1952. The Queen in half-mourning admires a brewery-gelding with Tom Forshaw in attendance.

way. Always calm. I never saw him put out by anything that ever happened. He never swore. Mr Jim could do a bit, though, and probably a good thing at times. One point about them two was they never ran anyone down, never criticised others. They'd sack a man, perhaps, but never pull him to bits afterwards. They were good living men, all of them, the Forshaws. At Carlton, you made a bargain, and didn't want any paper to write it on."

Charlie Butler, who became the outstanding man in the town-horse world, likewise spoke from an easy-chair. "Mr Tom must have been one of the greatest horsemen that ever lived. As a man, he was one in a hundred thousand. If he happened to be travelling by the Midland, then I'd have to drive him to Newark. You'd get to know a man a bit if you drove with him eight miles in a trap. He was a good man to be with, but he was always the same. I never saw his face change, even if the train was late. All those years I knew him, and that was fifty I suppose, he always looked the same. Immaculate, you know. Always wore a good suit, stiff collar and cuffs, boots polished, always fresh and clean, always in a state ready to meet the King. He was a wonderful man for system. When I was working there, everything was done at the same time every day, every week, every year. For instance, at seven o'clock every morning, he came out of the side door of his house. You'd know it was seven o'clock because his Pomeranian dog'd start barking. Some people said it was to let you know he

Fig. 49 Tom stepping out to give his casting vote at the National Foal
Show on 28th September 1955, three months before his death.

was coming, and perhaps they were right. It was certainly a useful warning.
He'd walk down the drive, and he'd go straight and see my uncle. Then he'd
go all round the boxes. Then he'd go in to breakfast. Then at nine o'clock he'd
be out again. System, that's what it was."

"He started off any number of other men, you know. Helped them begin,
gave them advice, watched how they went on. He never said anything about it,
but he'd love setting a man on the right road if he deserved it. And of course
the firm turned out a lot of good men, too, that went to other places. Take

Fig. 50 At least some good things have survived into
the present age! Charlie was the only employee of a
brewery, and the only professional horseman, whose
memorial is a pub named in his honour.

Johnson, for example. Anyone who can bring out a mare to be champion three
times, and then do it again with a stallion, is a bloody good man. That's what
Johnson did for Foster. And don't forget it was the Forshaws who set Foster
off by selling him his first Shires – and sending them Johnson."

"If Mr Tom had been a watchmaker, or something of that sort, he'd have
taken care he was the best bloody watchmaker in England. He was master of
himself. His life was so ordered he probably lay in one position all night. He
never changed his posture or his attitude. He didn't change whether he'd just
won the championship or just been beat – and there were plenty to remind him
of it, if he was. That was jealousy, but they thought of it as taking the micky.
Thomas Forshaw was a man who knew himself. He never showed what he
thought. He never voiced his opinions, except if anyone wanted to know. Then
he would, clearly and no disguise. His life was ruled by principle. Whether it
hurt or not, he always acted on his principle."

"Come to think of it, I did see him ruffled once. That was when his son was
killed. He said to me the next day, 'You've heard what happened?' So I said,

'Yes sir, and I'd like to say I am *very* sorry to hear it.' He then immediately read me a lecture. 'None of us ever knows,' he said 'what will happen, or whose turn it will be next. You must carefully study all that your uncle does – learn everything you can by watching him – observe every single *detail*. If he were to go, you'd have to be foreman, and if you're wise you'll learn all you can now. And that means every little point of the job.' 'Yes, sir,' I said. And that was the end of a conversation, which began with my trying to sympathise with a father who had just lost his son."

Tom Curtis, who had said that he would never leave Carlton for three times the money, never did. He was a good stockman and able foreman, though the only treatments he knew for recalcitrant engines were the boot and the hammer. Once he drove a Fordson tractor straight into a thick hedge at some speed because his natural instinct when disaster loomed close was to pull hard on the steering wheel and yell "Whoa back, whoa back". When Richard's second son Fred was of an age to ask him endless questions he sometimes liked to have his little joke, such as to tell him that in the First War he had served with the Underground Machine Gun Regiment or to present him with the shell of a bantam's egg to which the little boy gave pride of place on his bedroom mantelpiece and labelled "krokodil egg". Like many large and strong men, he was very amiable with children.

When he retired in 1959, he and Elsie remained in their house rent and rates free. "I called to see him most nights," Richard has said, "and he always wanted to know what we had been doing and to make suggestions. I greatly valued his advice. He was good company when we went to shows together and he had many friends, especially round Saffron Walden, where he travelled for so many years. He was a first class horseman, as his father had been. In June 1969 I was judging at the Essex Show. He asked me to look out for some of his old friends. This I did and told them all that he was fit and well and wished to be remembered to them. It was a great shock on my return to find that he had died, sitting quietly in his chair. He was a very sincere friend."

A true countryman, Curtis was fiercely patriotic. One does not meet many of his stamp today and when we are tempted to talk of the 'good old days' we should reflect that it is really not the days we mean, but the people who lived in them. He left two sons, both of whom, like Richard's three, were successful in a non-horse and non-agricultural world. The elder, John, had begun his career at the age of eighteen in the Palestine Police Force but later joined the Nottinghamshire Constabulary, as his father had been minded to do in 1919. He was its first dog handler and his Frankie enabled him to make his first arrest – of six escaped Rampton prisoners who were caught in a field of kale at the Carlton Stud farm. (He later transferred to the Metropolitan Police, where he rose to the rank of Chief Superintendent and eventually Commander.)

One day some years after Curtis' death, Richard was in Gainsborough and decided to visit old Jack Taylor. Enquiries led him to a little house at the bottom of a street. There was no one in, but there were pictures of horses on the walls. A neighbour said Mr Taylor could be found visiting his brother in a home. And there he was, sitting at another old man's side. Richard thought he would give him a surprise.

"Hello, Jack! Have you ever been back to Cornwall?"

What was intended as a cheerful greeting to put them both once again on the old familiar footing was unfortunately a nasty shock. Jack thought he had been hunted down at last. The import of his reply was "I've never been to Cornwall, and I don't know you. Whoever you are, clear out!"

It had not occurred to Richard that, after all this time, he might not be recognised. When he revealed his identity, it was all "I'm so sorry, sir. It is nice to see you, Mr Forshaw. But I should have known who you are. You sit in this chair, sir, please. And are you keeping well, Mr Forshaw? This is my brother Will."

The aged person that he indicated was the erstwhile randy one. His curly hair had gone now and his mumbled speech and rambling incoherence disguised his stutter. In course of conversation Jack confessed that, as a matter of fact, he had gone back, many years after, because curiosity got the better of him.

"I made enquiries. I knew the name to ask for. He had a fish and chip shop. So I went. I looked through the window. There was a youngish chap there. My God, sir. I thought I was looking in a mirror. The image of me like I used to be. A nice place he had. Married, with kids – I found that out. He was busy. I'd have liked to speak to him. My own son, you know. But I came away without a word spoken. Do you think I did right, Mr Forshaw?"

Richard reassured him and they talked of other things, such as Jack's experiences all over England getting horses ready for auction sales and his memories of customers in his sixteen years with the St Columb people – "there was some rum 'uns down there, you know, sir". But there was rum 'uns everywhere and the two had a good laugh, as Will sat there in a world of his own – thinking perhaps of when his father's trunk had been found full of sovereigns. As Richard took his leave, it was "Now you'll come again, won't you, Mr Forshaw?"

Index to the Forshaw Family

Relationships are to James (1840-1908) unless otherwise stated.

General Index

Names of horses are in italic. Only those mentioned more than once or of special significance are included. Names of individual stallion societies are in bold italic.